Proceedings of the
European Information Security Multi-Conference (EISMC 2013)

Lisbon, Portugal
8-10 May 2013

Editors

Steven Furnell
Nathan Clarke
Vasilis Katos

Centre for Security, Communications & Network Research
Plymouth University

ISBN: 978-1-84102-345-8

Preface

The European Information Security Multi-Conference (EISMC) brings together a series of established information security events into a single conference targeting today's information security practitioners, researchers and academics. Collectively addressing the issues human aspects of security, alongside a stream dedicated to digital investigation, the conference addresses the challenges of establishing, promoting and maintaining security, as well as addressing the difficulties that may be encountered when incidents occur and require analysis. The multi-conference is based upon the following contributing events:

- The 7th International Symposium on Human Aspects of Information Security and Assurance (HAISA);
- The 8th International Workshop on Digital Forensics and Incident Analysis (WDFIA).

Each of the contributing events has previously provided a respected forum for exchanging and sharing knowledge in key areas of the overall field of information security. Their combination within the context of this multi-conference is intended to enable an even wider opportunity for this to occur, enabling both academics and practitioners to review, present and discuss current research in their fields.

All of the papers were subject to double blind peer review, with each being reviewed by at least two members of the international programme committee. We have no doubt that the process yielded papers of high quality and we would like to thank the reviewers for their efforts in this regard.

We would like to thank the authors for submitting their work and sharing their findings, and the international programme committee for their efforts in reviewing the submissions and ensuring the quality of the resulting event and proceedings. We would also like to thank the local organising committee for making all the necessary arrangements to enable this conference to take place. Special thanks go to Gurpreet Dhillon, Mario Caldeira, Jesualdo Fernandes and Paul Dowland for their support with the underlying events within the multi-conference streams. Thanks are also due to Emerald (publishers of the sponsoring journal, *Information Management & Computer Security*) and the Colloquium for Information Systems Security Education (CISSE) as the co-sponsors of the event.

Steven Furnell, Nathan Clarke and Vasilis Katos
Conference Co-Chairs, EISMC 2013
Lisbon, May 2013

International Programme Committee

Helen Armstrong	Curtin University	Australia
Peter Bednar	University of Portsmouth	United Kingdom
Susan Brenner	University of Dayton	United States
William Buchanan	Napier University	United Kingdom
Ana Cerezo	University of Malaga	Spain
Jeff Crume	IBM	United States
Dorothy Denning	Naval Postgraduate School	United States
Ronald Dodge	United States Military Academy	United States
Paul Dowland	Plymouth University	United Kingdom
Jan Eloff	University of Pretoria	South Africa
Simone Fischer-Huebner	Karlstad University	Sweden
Chris Fuhrman	Ecole de Technologie Superieure	Canada
Sarah Gordon		United States
Stefanos Gritzalis	University of the Aegean	Greece
John Haggerty	University of Salford	United Kingdom
Chris Hargreaves	Cranfield University	United Kingdom
Cheryl Hennell	BT Openreach	United Kingdom
John Howie	Cloud Security Alliance	United States
William Hutchinson	Edith Cowan University	Australia
Christos Illioudis	ATEI of Thessalonki	Greece
Alastair Irons	University of Sunderland	United Kingdom
Murray Jennex	San Diego State University	United States
Andy Jones	Khalifa University of Science	UAE
	Edith Cowan University	Australia
Sevasti Karatzouni	University of Portsmouth	United Kingdom
Maria Karyda	University of Aegean	Greece
Tom Karygiannis	NIST	United States
Vasilios Katos	University of Portsmouth	United Kingdom
Sokratis Katsikas	University of Piraeus	Greece
Gary Kessler	Champlain College	United States
Spyros Kokolakis	University of the Aegean	Greece
Igor Kotenko	SPIIRAS	Russia
David Lacey	David Lacey Consulting	United Kingdom
Costas Lambrinoudakis	University of Piraeus	Greece
Michael Lavine	John Hopkins University	United States
Chang-Tsun Li	University of Warwick	United Kingdom
Javier Lopez	University of Malaga	Spain
Thomas Martin	Khalifa University	UAE
Ian Mitchell	Middlesex University	United Kingdom
Lillian Mitrou	University of the Aegean	Greece
Martin Olivier	University of Pretoria	South Africa
Maria Papadaki	Plymouth University	United Kingdom
Ahmed Patel	University of Kebangsaan	Malaysia
Malcolm Pattinson	University of Adelaide	Australia
Gunther Pernul	University of Regensburg	Germany
Gerald Quirchmayr	University of Vienna	Austria
Corey Schou	Idaho State University	United States
Rossouw von Solms	Nelson Mandela Metropolitan University	South Africa

Jeffrey Stanton	Syracuse University	United States
Hatem Tamman	Staffordshire University	United Kingdom
Paula Thomas	University of Glamorgan	United Kingdom
Kerry-Lynn Thomson	Nelson Mandela Metropolitan University	South Africa
Theodore Tryfonas	University of Bristol	United Kingdom
Craig Valli	Edith Cowan University	Australia
Kim Vu	California State University	United States
Jeremy Ward	HP Enterprise Security	United Kingdom
Merrill Warkentin	Mississippi State University	United States
Matthew Warren	Deakin University	Australia
Louise Yngstrom	Stockholm University	Sweden
Mary Ellen Zurko	Cisco	United States

Contents

Chapter 1

Human Aspects of Information Security and Assurance

Shrinking the Authentication Footprint

K. Renaud and J. Maguire

School of Computing Science, University of Glasgow
e-mail: karen.renaud@glasgow.ac.uk

Abstract

Developers create paths for users to tread. Some users will stay on the beaten track; others will diverge and take risky shortcuts. If user-preferred and developer-created paths diverge too much, it is time for the developer to consider a new path. A case in point is the humble password. They fill an important developer need: a cheap and easy mechanism to control access and enforce accountability. Unfortunately, users find the constant requests for authentication a nuisance. They respond by walking down risky paths that compromise the mechanism but allow them to satisfy goals more quickly. The answer, for some researchers, has been to come up with password alternatives. This focus is misguided, since the alternatives do nothing to reduce the authentication footprint. The reality is that developers overuse authentication. The problem is not the authentication step, but rather its position in the path. Authentication is sometimes used even when there is no real need for it. This creates confusion in the user's mind about the consequences of authentication: sometimes it authorises significant side effects and other times it is difficult to identify its *raison d'etre*. Here we suggest some developer patterns which minimise authentication requests, emphasising necessity rather than gratuitousness. We believe this will help to ease the current situation by moving towards genuine risk mitigation rather than harming authentication by excessive use thereof.

Keywords

Authentication, Patterns, Password

1. Introduction

Researchers have spent a great deal of effort coming up with new authentication mechanisms eg. alternative alphanumeric approaches (Zviran & Haga, 1990), graphical alternatives (Jermyn et al., 1999) and even audible passwords (Gibson et al, 2009). The motivation appears to be to find a more memorable alternative to supplant the password. Having found one, researchers publish details, with evidence of the alternative mechanism's superiority. Yet the password persists.

The widespread use of passwords has accustomed users to access control as a necessary evil. Unfortunately, the very familiarity of the mechanism has also been its undoing. A clear indication of the failure of the password is the prevalence of policies and procedures that use words such as "comply", "sanction" and "disciplinary". Unfortunately these policies, instead of convincing users to walk the developer's intended path, often do more harm than good (Herley, 2009).

As authentication researchers, we have often been obsessed by the mechanism itself, rather than its placement within a workflow, task or path. Developers define such workflows and lay down paths for navigating them, users merely react. Hence *developers* determine the position, use and frequency of authentication challenges. We need first to understand their perspective, the paths they create, and how these can better be designed to overlap with paths users prefer.

2. Developer Survey

We carried out a survey of software developers to find out what their concerns were with respect to authentication, and alternative approaches, and to assess the level of awareness of alternatives. 89 developers responded to our survey, of whom 71% developed systems for the desktop, 26% developed for mobile environments and the rest developed for both. 33% had had some experience of authentication other than the password although 73% were aware that alternatives to passwords existed.

We asked *"When you need to restrict access, what do you usually use?"*. 70% of respondents referred to an identifier/password combination. Two mentioned the use of Lotus auto-authentication, a number simply said "ADS" and three said that they would use device id in conjunction with the identifier and password. One mentioned using a fingerprint and one a token. For this group, the password seemed the most popular authentication choice.

A number of questions were asked about password use, use of alternatives, context of use etc. These questions were designed to elicit open-ended responses. The responses were analysed using a Grounded Theory approach. We wanted themes to emerge rather than using an approach which utilised a-priori themes. First all responses were examined and acceptance-related aspects coded, then codes were grouped into emerging themes.

The first question asked whether respondents thought there were contexts where passwords were unsuitable. A number of themes emerged from their responses in terms of context. (A1) unsuitability for users, either in terms of accessibility or memory; (A2) where the authentication was happening: in public, where people could be observed, and on a single-user device; (A3) what data/application was being protected; (A4) acceptability by users/enterprise.

We asked whether they would consider using a graphical mechanism if it were proven suitable for their user group. Here recurring themes were: (B1) strength of the mechanism; (B2) accessibility and memorial issues; (B3) implementation and deployment concerns; (B4) acceptability.

The final question asked what factors would need to be in place for developers to consider switching to another mechanism. Here the themes were: (C1) Cost of the mechanism and the value to the enterprise; (C2) Provable strength; (C3) Evidence of use of the mechanism by others, and empirical evidence of efficacy; (C4) usability and accessibility for users; (C5) ease of implementation and deployment.

We derived the following meta-themes (Figure 1):

Risk: matching the mechanism to the asset being protected
(A2, A3, B1, C2);
Users: ensuring that users will be able to use and accept mechanism
(A1, B2, B4, C4);
Value: cost of implementation and switch and associated value to enterprise
(B3, C1, C5);
Evidence: being able to assess whether other users/enterprises have
accepted and used the mechanism
(A4, C3).

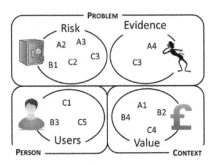

Figure 1: Developers' Perspectives

Bettman (1991) models consumer intentions to adopt online shopping based on three factors: *person, problem* and *context*. Bettman's model was confirmed fifteen years later, after online shopping had become far more common-place, by Moon (2004). What emerged from our analysis was also the *person* (users), the *problem* (choosing a mechanism based on perceived risk and evidence to provide confirmation) and the *context* (value to the organisation). Finally, one comment seems to summarise what many of the respondents were saying:

"Passwords are lame with many downsides... but they are mature, time-tested, and people/organizations are comfortable with them... Any alternatives will need to spend a lot of time gaining mindshare in both the user and enterprise world before it can be adopted... For a fundamental security concept like passwords, "The beast that you know" is definitely better..."

The survey provided responses that highlighted themes of concern related to switching to an alternative form of authentication even though awareness of alternatives was fairly high. It is instructive to consider how the current authentication paths came into being.

3. Paths in the Grass

Siracusa (2006) talks about users making "paths in the grass": paths which allow them to achieve their goals while expending as little extraneous effort as possible. He says:

*"Any viable solution must work within the (often inconvenient) bounds of reality. It must be constructed in such a way that the motivations and actions of the participants—both the good and the bad...*especially *the bad—serve to **balance** the system as a whole. Suggesting that all would be well, if only certain people would act differently or alter their desires in some way is wishful thinking, not an actual solution."*

This strikes a chord. Wishing that people *"would only behave securely"* has almost been the mantra of security practitioners world-wide for at least the last decade. Siracusa argues that socialism, communism and libertarianism have failed because they attempt to create artificial systems which ignore the nature of participants, or which insist that they change their nature.

Siracusa relates that when the University of California at Irvine campus was first built, they did not lay sidewalks: they planted grass. The next year, they returned and laid the sidewalks where the trails were in the grass. We must find ways to consider *how* users want to authenticate, and design to accommodate their "paths". Trying to coerce them into walking down our paths is futile.

Consider Wikipedia, a collaborative encyclopaedia launched shortly after the millennium. The articles on the website are generated by the man and woman in the street, not by experts. Wikipedia is the 6th most visited website on the planet[1]. The authors are not owners of articles *per se*: instead articles are generated through user collaboration, by crowd-sourcing. Users are not vetted; any individual is able to generate or edit an article. In summary, Wikipedia's developers had *people* (everyone), *problem* (building a knowledge resource), and *context* (accountability is less important than encouraging contributions). They chose a novel approach: no authentication.

Malicious users are always a concern and the obvious solution would have been to require authentication. Yet that would probably have discouraged contributors, and Wikipedia seemingly wanted to be sure that no obstacles impeded the creation of a knowledge resource, so they created a new "path" of unhindered access. It turns out that the developers' path coincided with the path users preferred, as demonstrated by the efforts of millions of contributors. Investigations have found the pages to be of high quality (Giles, 2005) similar to traditional encyclopaedias. Vandalism attacks do occur (Viegas, 2004) but users are unaware of this because tools, such as watchlists (Nasaw, 2012), make contributors aware of changes so that they can be corrected. Wikipedia has essentially outsourced both creation and policing. Their approach perfectly matches the risk problems of their context, and it works. Wikipedia's approach is unusual. Let us consider where traditional password usage originated.

---

[1] Alexa. Wikipedia Traffic Information. January
2013.http://www.alexa.com/siteinfo/wikipedia.org?range=5y&size=large&y=t

3.1. Antecedents

For many of us, the paths we tread are historical, informed by tradition and a sense that "I have always done it that way". In the academic literature this is referred to as path dependency, the view that technological change in a society depends on its own past. (Shalizi, 2001; David, (1985, 2000)).

The digital password was designed for professionals and originally surfaced in a system designed to empower professionals in 1962 (Corbato, 1962). The password approach was used to enforce access control.

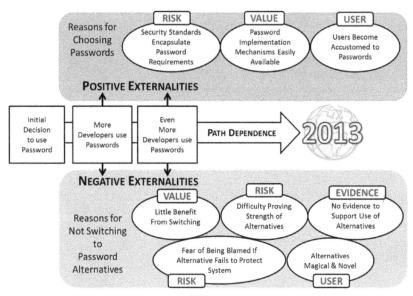

Figure 2: Progress and Path Dependence of Passwords

The current situation, in terms of authentication, is a perfect example of path dependency (Figure 2). This path exhibits extreme dependency on the initial condition (Page, 2006). The initial choice for authentication was the password. This led to operating systems incorporating a password mechanism, and making this available for use by developers. It is a well-understood paradigm, and password rules and requirements are encoded in various security standards. Most importantly, users are comfortable with the *concept* of passwords. They have grown up with stories about Ali Baba and the 40 thieves. The use of passwords throughout history in a military context has familiarised the general populace with the concept, and it is not difficult for them to understand. These are termed positive externalities by Page (2006). There are some negative externalities as well. Our society tends to identify a scapegoat when things go wrong, and this is an unenviable position to be in. "Accountability" is the flavour of the day, and many act defensively and conservatively to ensure that they will not become the focus of rancour.

Choosing a password to protect a system is an approved and widely-used mechanism. There was a saying in the 1970s and 1980s that *"no one is fired for buying IBM*". Today no one can get fired for using a password. Even if one were to find a developer willing to use an alternative, how would he or she convince the other stakeholders? There is little convincing evidence of the strength of alternatives: most research effort has gone into demonstrating their superior memorability and usability. So, whereas there is significant personal risk in switching and a powerful self-protecting motive to use passwords, it is unsurprising that the password still pervades.

Hence the password has prevailed, not as the outcome of scientific experiments which found it to be optimal, but rather as a consequence of compromises, *ad hoc* decisions and hardware affordances. Many of the problems which have emerged over the last years are a direct consequence of their extensive use and deployment. Corbato stated that although passwords had seemed theoretically sound, in practice flaws became apparent (Corbato, 1990). Corbato's comments have been echoed numerous times by a number of researchers in the authentication area, not to speak of security practitioners and end users.

Passwords, in 2013, are more aligned to the aims and perspectives of the security lobby than human requirements. The developer path has deviated from the paths users would like to tread. The result appears to be an impasse.

Boas (2007) argues that changes to entrenched technologies will only occur if they are replaced wholesale, by a disruptive technology. He suggests that the Sholes QWERTY keyboard, for example, might be replaced by voice recognition, but not by another keyboard, even if the new keyboard is superior. Password practice has worn deep furrows into the landscape. Authentication researchers have been striving towards finding the disruptive technology which will effect this replacement. It is time to step back and reconsider our assumptions and approach.

The reality is that the password will probably be around, in the same format, a decade from now (Herley *et al.*, 2009). Herley *et al.* argue that researchers have failed to realise that the password *is* actually the best authentication solution in many contexts. The password is powerful, accessible and versatile (O'Gorman, 2003). Passwords, in their first incarnation, performed exactly as planned. Many of the problems we have today are a direct consequence of indiscriminate and excessive usage thereof. Consequently, rather than attempting to replace the password, a near-term solution may be to accept it but to find a better way of mediating its use, of tackling the gratuitousness of password usage.

3.2. Usage Paths

The password, as a general concept, has a historical path dependency. There are also usage paths in how passwords have been applied by developers. Authentication is essentially used as a gateway, to mediate all access, both risky and innocuous. Once authenticated, the verified individual is free to perform any action at will. This can be depicted as shown in Figure 3. This pattern dictates that users authenticate in order to use the device or application. Having done so, they can carry out any of the mediated actions on the device or within the application.

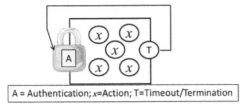

A = Authentication; *x*=Action; T=Timeout/Termination

Figure 3: Gateway Authentication Pattern

This password positioning pattern is historical, and harks back to the era of shared desktop computers. These are far less common than they used to be. Nowadays most employees have dedicated desktop or mobile computers: essentially their own devices. Moreover, if the computer is located within an unshared secured office space then the device is secured by other means: requiring device-oriented authentication becomes gratuitous and wasteful. Moreover, such binary access does not deliver the kind of nuanced access within applications that could be delivered. It is generally recognised that activities have associated and diverse risk levels. Some are easily reversed, and others have side effects which cannot be remediated. To apply one authentication mechanism, which we know to have flaws, to permit activities of wide-ranging risk categories seems rather *passé*.

Developers have failed to accommodate the emergent changing *user context*. The following section presents patterns that position authentication to accommodate the emergent user context of the 21st century.

4. Developer Usage Patterns

Here we present authentication usage patterns that would serve to reduce the deployment of authentication to sufficiency rather than extravagance. It is worth considering how many times an individual is required actively to unlock their device during any given day. They may infrequently perform actions with serious or risky side-effects. Nevertheless, whether or not they want to use their device to check the time or to stop music playing, they are presented with an authentication hurdle. This traditional approach can be referred to as "exhaustive access control". Consider that we could categorise actions, rather coarsely, as follows:

1. *No Risk*: No side effects, including actions such as playing music, carrying out a web search, or consulting the system calendar.

2. *Some or Major Risk*: Access sensitive information, or initiate significant side effects such as, for example, making a purchase on an ecommerce site, or accessing email.

Hence we can introduce a new pattern which positions authentication differently. Our proposal for a more prudent access control pattern would be that a user can carry out any no-risk activity without authenticating but if they want to carry out a risky activity, they have to authenticate first (after which all risky activities are permitted).

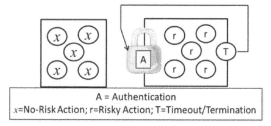

A = Authentication
x=No-Risk Action; r=Risky Action; T=Timeout/Termination

Figure 4: Risk Categorisation Authentication Pattern

The advantage of this pattern is that authentication is used only when necessary. In so doing it fosters a clear connection in the user's mind between authentication and significant consequences. This pattern makes it possible to match the strength of the authentication to the significance/riskiness of the authorised action and to use a bespoke authenticator for different applications. Why would developers use this pattern? It depends on their analysis of the risk. If they are able to separate activities within their application into those that create no harmful side effects, and those that do, then this pattern would be especially beneficial in increasing usage. This pattern is already applied by canny e-commerce sites, such as Amazon. They only authenticate for purchases or to access personal information. All other actions proceed unhindered. Email, which does not support such categorisation, requires a traditional authentication gateway approach.

We can take this a step further. Consider that we could split category 2 (risky) above into two sub-categories: (2a): Has side effects which are easily reversed; and (2b): Has side effects which are difficult or costly to reverse. Email and purchases of goods that need to be delivered physically are an example of 2b. An example of the former is digital media purchases. Digital goods, for the most part, are tightly controlled using digital rights management (DRM) and their use is heavily restricted. Individual purchases are generally tied to a specific account and set of devices.

For 2a, we could put the focus on compensating transactions rather than prevention. The techniques used by Wikipedia to preserve articles, coupled with DRM, could be used to remove the need for an authentication step and still mitigate risk. The user's device acts as a token removing the need for explicit authentication. Users discovering unauthorised purchases could report this and DRM used to remotely deactivate disputed digital goods. Watchlists could be deployed, as in Wikipedia, to improve the ability of the digital content providers to uncover fraudulent behaviours. Hence we have a third pattern. Users can carry out a no-risk or a compensatable activity without authenticating, but once they wish to carry out an action with significant side-effects they have to authenticate. (Figure 5)

This pattern is more fine-grained than the previous one and clearly only applies in particular contexts. However, we need to be creative in finding ways to reduce unnecessary authentication, and this is a relatively simple way of achieving it. Why would developers want to use this pattern? Because humans always act to minimise effort (Zipf, 1949), so removing hurdles encourages action and will probably lead to increased sales and application usage.

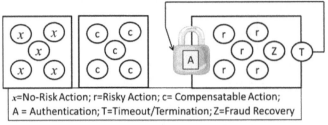

x=No-Risk Action; r=Risky Action; c= Compensatable Action;
A = Authentication; T=Timeout/Termination; Z=Fraud Recovery

Figure 5: Minimal Authentication Pattern

What about lost or stolen devices? Device authentication, as implemented on most devices, offers little resistance to a determined thief. Using our pattern ensures that only no-risk and compensatable actions could be performed. The owner would then deactivate the device with companies he/she usually purchases electronic goods from and the thief will be unable to use the device to defraud the original owner.

5. Conclusion

The problems of passwords are not necessary insurmountable or bad enough to warrant instant replacement. In the near-time we can make changes in patterns to get more life out the password. Here we have provided two alternative usage patterns which will ease overuse while still accommodating the needs of risk mitigation. Our patterns fit better into a 21st century context of single-owner and single-user devices, accommodating human path preferences.

6. References

Bettman, J.R., Johnson, E.J. and Payne, J.W. (1990), "A componential analysis of cognitive effort in choice", *Organizational Behavior and Human Decision Processes*, Vol. 41,pp93–110.

Boas, T. C. (2007), "Conceptualizing Continuity and Change: The Composite-Standard Model of Path Dependence", *Journal of Theoretical Politics*, Vol. 19, No. 1, pp33-54.

Corbato, F.J. (1990), "On building systems that will fail" In ACM Turing Award Lectures. ACM.

Corbato, F.J., Merwin-Daggett, M. and Daley, R.C. (1962), "An Experimental Time-sharing System", In: *Proceedings of the Spring Joint Computer Conference*, San Francisco, California. May 1-3. pp335-344. ACM.

Norman, D. A. and Fisher, D. (1982), "Why Alphabetic Keyboards Are Not Easy to Use: Keyboard Layout Doesn't Much Matter" *Human Factors: The Journal of the Human Factors and Ergonomics Society*, Vol. 24, No. 5, pp509-519.

David, P. A. (1985), "Clio and the Economics of QWERTY", *American Economic Review*, Vol. 75, No. 2, pp332–37.

David, P. (2000), "Path dependence, its critics and the quest for 'historical economics'", In P. Garrouste and S. Ioannides (eds), Evolution and Path Dependence in Economic Ideas: Past and Present, Edward Elgar Publishing, Cheltenham, England.

Flechais, I., Sasse, M. A. and Hailes, S. (2003), "Bringing security home: a process for developing secure and usable systems" In *Proceedings of the 2003 workshop on New security paradigms*, Ascona, Switzerland, 18-21 August, pp49–57, ACM.

Gibson, M., Renaud, K. and Conrad, M. (2009), "Authenticating me softly with "my" song" *Proceedings of the 2009 workshop on New security paradigms*. The Queen's College University of Oxford, UK, September 8-11, pp85-100

Giles, J. (2005), "Internet encyclopaedias go head to head", *Nature,* Vol. 438, pp900-901

Herley, C. van Oorschot, P. and Patrick, A. (2009), "Passwords: If we're so smart, why are we still using them?" *Financial Cryptography and Data Security*, Accra Beach: Barbados, February, pp230–237.

Herley, C. (2009), "So long, and no thanks for the externalities: the rational rejection of security advice by users" In *Proceedings of the 2009 workshop on New security paradigms workshop*, The Queen's College University of Oxford, UK, September 8-11, pp133–144.

Herley, C. and Van Oorschot, P. (2012), "A research agenda acknowledging the persistence of passwords" *IEEE Security & Privacy*, Vol. 10, No. 1, pp28–36.

Jermyn, I. Mayer, A. Monrose, F., Reiter, M. and Rubin, A. (1999), "The Design and Analysis of Graphical Passwords", In *Proceedings of the 8th USENIX Security Symposium*, Washington DC, 23-26 August, pp1–14.

Moon, B-J. (2004), "Consumer adoption of the internet asan information search and product purchase channel: some research hypotheses", *Int. J. Internet Marketing and Advertising*, Vol. 1, No. 1, pp104–118.

Nasaw, D. (2012), Meet the 'bots' that edit Wikipedia. *BBC News Magazine*. http://www.bbc.co.uk/news/magazine-18892510

O'Gorman, L. (2003), "Comparing passwords, tokens, and biometrics for user authentication" In: *Proceedings of the IEEE*, Vol. 91, No. 12, pp2021–2040.

Page, S. E. (2006), "Path Dependence", *Quarterly Journal of Political Science*, Vol. 1, pp87-115.

Shalizi, C. (2001), "QWERTY, Lock-in, and Path Dependence", unpublished website (http://cscs.umich.edu/~crshalizi/notebooks/qwerty.html), with extensive references

Siracusa, J. (2006), "Paths in the grass. We have created, for the first time in all history, a garden of pure ideology" http://arstechnica.com/staff/2006/02/2918/

Wurster, G. and van Oorschot, P. (2008), "The developer is the enemy" In *Proceedings of the 2008 workshop on New security paradigms*, Lake Tahoe, CA, September 22-25, pp89–97.

Zipf, G. K. (1949) *Human behavior and the principle of least effort*. Oxford, England: Addison-Wesley Press.

Zviran, M. and Haga, W. (1990), "Cognitive Passwords: The Key to Easy Access Control", *Computers & Security*, Vol. 9, No. 8, pp723–736.

Contextualized Security Interventions in Password Transmission Scenarios

M. Volkamer, S. Bartsch and M. Kauer

CASED, Technische Universität Darmstadt, Germany
e-mail: name.surname@cased.de

Abstract

Usable security user studies as well as the number of successful attacks to end users' data and devices show that today's security interventions like the green URL bar and self-signed certificate warnings do not protect end users effectively for many reasons. To improve the situation, we proposed the Framework fOr Contextualized security Interventions (FOCI). While this framework provides general guidelines how to develop contextualized security interventions, this is the first paper in which this framework is applied to actually develop adequate security intervention strategies and intervention content. We focus on a subset of security- and privacy-critical scenarios in the context of web applications – namely those in which users visit web pages containing a password filed. If either the communication is not confidential and authenticated or the service behind the web page is not trustworthy, entering a password can have consequences like financial loss and privacy leakage in particular for users reusing their passwords for several different web pages. Therefore, it is important to provide effective security interventions for these scenarios.

Keywords

Security intervention, human aspects, contextualized, https, secure password transmission, intervention strategy, threats, consequences, risks.

1. Introduction

Many user studies and statistics concerning successful attacks against end users show that neither current passive interventions (like the green URL bar in case of an extended SSL certificate) nor (active warnings like those in cased of self-signed certificates) do effectively protect their users (Dhamija *et al.* 2006, Sunshine *et al.* 2009). Researchers have identified several reasons. The main reason is that existing interventions do not adequately take into account that security is not their primary task but e.g. transferring money or buying books (West 2008, Sasse *et al.* 2001) and that the user's mental model and knowledge of Internet security is incomplete (Bravo-Lillo *et al.* 2011b). For instance, many users believe that they personally are not of interest for an attacker (Sasse *et al.* 2012). Studies also show that people tend to base the decision whether to use or not to use a web page on the design of the web page and not on (passive) security interventions (Fogg *et al.* 2001, Schechter *et al.* 2006). In general one can say that existing passive security interventions are not noticed by most of the users. Active security interventions interrupt users from their primary task and can therefore not be overlooked. However, active warnings are not much more effective for many reasons; as for instances Sunshine *et al.* (2009) show. One problem is that the communicated information about the situation or reason for this intervention is currently on a very technical level. Thus, users are not able to deduce the risk and their personal consequences of ignoring this intervention from the provided information (Bravo-Lillo *et al.* 2011a and Kauer *et at.* 2012). In combination with the fact that browsers show the same security interventions in high and in low risk situations, users learned from many low risk situations in their daily lives that nothing "bad" happens if they ignore these interventions (Sotirakopoulos *et al.* 2011, Sunshine *et al.* 2009). Correspondingly, it is not surprising that - due to habituation effects - users will also ignore such interventions in high risk situations.

In order to improve the situation, Bartsch and Volkamer (2012) proposed the Framework fOr Contextualized security Interventions (FOCI). The main idea is that the appearance of an intervention (intervene or not), the time, type and position of the intervention (all this is defined in the intervention strategy), and the content of an intervention is primarily influenced by the user's context. The context is defined by the user's personal characteristics and the situation (what do we know about the web page, the connection to the web server, and the operator of the web page or web service). The authors left it for future work to operationalize this very general framework with respect to the different existing security-critical contexts.

In this paper, we focus on security-critical scenarios in the context of web pages with password fields (e.g. password requests over http or over https with self-signed certificates) and describe the proposed algorithm to determine whether to intervene and how (passive or active, as well as position). The reason to start with these scenarios is, on the one hand, that many of the common phishing attacks are covered with these scenarios and, on the other hand, the fact that many users reuse passwords between different services. Consequently, being able to "phish" one password often enables the attacker to get access to several web services. The proposed interventions strategy combines and extends existing approaches for security interventions; namely the multi-page warning approach proposed by Sunshine *et al.* (2009) and extended by Seikel (2012) and the idea from Maurer *et al.* (2011a and b) to display warnings only if the user starts entering sensitive data and place the warning right where the data is entered.

2. Framework for Contextualized security Interventions

The main idea of the framework proposed by Bartsch and Volkamer (2012) is that the intervention strategy including the appearance of an intervention (intervene or not), the time, type and position of the intervention (all this is defined in the intervention strategy), as well as the content of an intervention is primarily influenced by the concrete *situation* and *personal characteristics* (see Figure 1).

Situation indicators include *security-related indicators* which enable the framework to measure the security in a particular situation based on indicators like the trustworthiness of the operator of the web service, the protection of the communication path to the web service, the requested data (e.g. passwords, credit cards or other sensible data), the type of web page (information pages versus online banking), the user's intention (whether to provide this data or not), and whether the user visited the same URL already in past. Other situation indicators are so called *user-influencing indicators*. Examples are professional design or containing logos from trustworthy institutions but also the type of web page and the requested data. **Personal characteristics** include the user's demographics, user's mental model and knowledge of Internet and computer/mobile security as well as his risk profile. The risk profile defines the readiness to assume a risk in different situations.

The framework requires an interdisciplinary collaboration from security and psychology researchers in order to deduce adequate contextualized intervention strategies and content. Thereby, FOCI includes results from Sunshine *et al.* (2009) and Cranor (2008). Sunshine *et al.* (2009) already indicate that the effectiveness of warnings can be improved, if the content and the intensity are adjusted to the specific context, while context in their paper mainly includes the type of web page the user visits. Cranor proposed (2008) a human-in-the-loop security framework, which describes which factors influence users, namely "personal variables" such as the user's demographics, "intentions" as the user's attitudes and believe, and "capabilities" for the user's knowledge or cognitive and physical skills. Correspondingly, also according to Cranor (2008) different warnings are necessary.

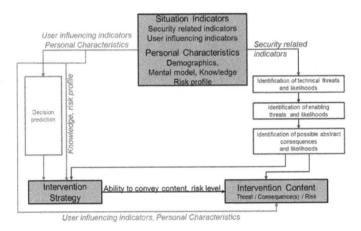

Figure 1: Framework for contextualized Security Interventions

FOCI should support developers in developing an *algorithm* to deduce for individual situations and users the appropriated intervention strategy and the appropriate content if an intervention is displayed which allows conveying content. Such an algorithm can either be integrated in future Browsers or available as an add-on.

As input for the algorithm both disciplines need to *identify and weigh relevant situation indicators and personal characteristics*, respectively. Based on these indicators the psychologists develop an algorithm *to predict the user's decision* without any further intervention (the idea is not to replace existing passive interventions, like the green URL bar). The idea is to only confront the user with additional passive or active interventions if the user would make an unintentional risky decision without. Security experts need to develop algorithms to deduce the overall *risk level, possible abstract consequences and their likelihoods* based on the identified security related indicators. Bartsch and Volkamer (2012) recommend to conduct user studies, literature reviews and to consult experts both to identify and weighing situation indicators and personal characteristics. In addition, for each of the situation indicators, researchers need to define how these indicators can be deduced. It is recommended that ideally the user is only involved in the setup phase of such a tool by answering some questions concerning his personal characteristics and web pages he has accounts for. Note, already in this stage such a tool would check whether the provided URLs/domains are critical with respect to password transmissions. Therefore, after the setup phase, it can be assumed that on these web pages either no problem exists or the user accepts this risk.

Correspondingly, situation indicators are ideally automatically deduced when visiting a web page. In Bartsch and Volkamer (2012), it is recommended to conduct a cost benefit analysis when thinking of involving the user in determining situation indicators, e.g. by asking him what type of web page he tries to access or whether he plans to login on this page. Correspondingly, it is recommended to first evaluate all the situation indicators which can automatically be determined and all information from the setup phase. Then it needs to be decided whether the intervention strategy and content can be based on this information or whether additional information is required to support the user adequately. As the number of possible combinations of situation indicators and personal characteristics is large, it is recommended to start with concrete scenarios. In this paper we operationalized a first set of concrete scenarios, that is, visiting web pages with password requests (password fields appear on the web page). We focus on the strategy rather than on the content.

3. Adapted approaches for proposed strategy

For the operationalization of our framework we integrate, combine, adapt, and refine the results from the following papers: In 2009, Sunshine *et al.* introduced the concept of multi-page warnings. The idea is, once the browser detects a security risk, a first dialog asks the user which type of web page he wants to visit. Depending on his choice, the user is either shown a warning or not. With this multi-page warning approach, the authors wanted to achieve, that the warning is only shown if the user stated that he wants to reach a web page with a higher criticality (which was either "Bank or other financial institution" or "Online store or other e-commerce website"). One main result of the study is that multi-page warnings are a promising approach for future frameworks. Seikel, (2012) extended this work by systematically identifying a set of seven web page categories for the dialog. The author further proposes to provide the user the option to store this assignment of the corresponding URL. In addition, it is proposed that, if the user selects the option 'information web pages' but, then he, later on, tries to login on this page, he is warned again.

The second promising approach in improving the effectiveness of browser security warnings, in particular in the context of phishing, was proposed by Maurer *et al.* in (2011a and b). The main idea is to only show the warning when the user starts entering sensitive data and at the precise spot of the browser where the data is entered. Note, their plug-in disables the original SSL browser warnings. Thus the user is able to visit web pages without being warned even if the browser detects any problems with SSL. Showing these so called "semi-blocking" warnings is a very interesting approach, while it underlies the same problem as the passive security indicators: Namely, if the 'look and feel' of the web page appeals to the user, it is more likely that he will continue entering sensitive data, despite the warning as shown by Gutmann (2011).

4. Situation indicators and personal characteristics

In this section, situation indicators and relevant personal characteristics are identified. Furthermore, it is explained how these indicators can be deduced.

Security related indicators. In order to identify the possible consequences and the risk in a particular situation, we need to identify first the relevant security related indicators for the considered password transmission scenarios. We systematically reviewed important security, Web, and HCI conferences for papers on Web security measures and identified the following security indicators:

- contains password field: Yes / No?
- https: Yes / No?
- valid certificate: Yes / No?
- self-signed: Yes / No?
- CA known: Yes / No?
- trustworthiness rating from external services for this web page such as Web of Trust, McAfee SiteAdvisor, and google safe browsing.

In order to deduce possible (enabling) threats and consequences as well as the risk level the following information is required according to the literature:

- User's intention to login
- Type of web page: Seikel (2012) systematically deduced the following seven types which we use for this paper: Information Site, Shopping, Online Banking, Social Network, Email, Data Exchange, and Others.

While the first list of security indicators can be automatically deduced, the last two indicators are more difficult to elaborate on. In worse case the user would be bothered with two corresponding questions whenever visiting a web page containing a password field and failing for any of the other security related indicators. Obviously, these costs are too high as users would be very likely to uninstall the tool. However, the tool can take the list of web pages listed in the setup phase into account and assuming that he only logs in on these pages. Furthermore, it can learn from previous actions (including creating new accounts) or decisions of a user on particular web pages, i.e. store this information in a history. Thus, once the user has answered the question about user's intention and type of web page for a particular URL or domain, this is stored and is used as input next time the same web page is visited. This reduces the number of interactions a lot. Therefore, we consider the

- 'URL/domain – login – web page type' history as further security related indicator.

Furthermore, *natural language processing* (NLP) techniques are proposed to be integrated to deduce the type of web page. Note, such a solution would in some cases come to its limits: For instance 'www.google.com' provides many different services, with different criticalities and different consequences. For example, on the one hand Google can only be used as a search engine, and on the other hand it provides email services and a social network.

User influencing indicators. We systematically reviewed important security, Web, and HCI conferences for papers on user influencing factors. The main user influencing factor (if no warning is shown) is the design of the page (Fogg *et al.* 2001, Schechter *et al.* 2006). Furthermore, (Fogg *et al.* 2001) showed that user consider the type of web page. However, the type has not necessarily an influence in the same direction; i.e. some users are more concerned and more careful on e-banking pages as others are less because they for instance believe the bank takes care of their security. Similar to the type of web page it also has an influence whether the user knows the company. Correspondingly, the user influencing indicators are:

- Design of the web page (similarity to known pages, general design)
- Type of web page
- User knows the company/service

In order to get the impression about the design and thereby the trustworthiness of this particular user it would be necessary to ask the user. As the costs are obviously too high to ask him for each web page potentially causing threats and containing a password field, this needs to be automatically deduced (as far as possible and even if this will not exactly match to the user's impression). We propose to analyse whether the web page looks similar to one of the pages the user has an account at (known from the setup phase or the history) and take this similarity aspect as user influencing indicator. In addition, we propose to extend web accessibility evaluation tools to use them to automatically deduce the general design quality of the web page.

The challenges and possible solutions to deduce the web page type, we discussed already with the security related indicators and refer the reader there.

Which companies are known by the individual user can only be answered by the user itself. Of course one can consider here again those pages he has an account at (from the setup phase and history). In addition, one could think of the TOP 100 visited web pages but it is not known whether these are also known to most of the popularity. Correspondingly, we propose to only take companies from the setup phase and the history into account to decide whether someone knows this company/service or not.

Personal characteristics. The effect each influencing factor has (more likely to ignore intervention or not) depends on the personal characteristics. According to the literature these are age, education, ownership, Internet/security knowledge, Internet usage (which applications, since when, and how often), and number of web-enabled devices; as well as situation specific once: namely the perceived risk, expected benefit, and the rating of expected risk. This is obviously a rather complicated field. Thus, we take only scenario specific characteristics into account which are:

- Risk ranking of different web page types (as part of their mental model)
- Knowledge about passwords

We propose the following approach to collect this information: users are ask in the setup phase to sort different web page types according to the risk they perceive if someone else has access to their account on this web page. In addition, users are asked to participate in a small quiz in order to distinguish between experts and laypersons; while experts are those who know about the consequences if passwords are transmitted unencrypted or to an unauthorized service; and who use different and where recommended secure passwords. This will result in a very small group of experts however for the strategy whether to interfere or not it should be sufficient to distinguish these two groups. If we later also consider the type of intervention then we might need to distinguish between more groups. Note, the development of such a quiz as well as the question whether more groups are adequate is left for future work.

5. Weighing security related indicators and decision prediction

Threats, Consequences, and Risk. Assuming, all the security related indicators can be determined (automatically or by asking), then according to FOCI, the next step is to deduce possible (enabling) threats and consequences as well as objective risk levels. Note, we consider here only those URLs that are not contained in the setup list and not in the history file. Those are treated differently: The tool only intervenes if one of the security-relevant indicators changes.

We propose in Table 1 **risk** levels for different results for different security-critical indicators while assuming we know the user's intention is to login (L – Low, M – Medium, H – High, and X is the risk level according to the other services). If more than one of the five indicators about the connection to the server and the server itself fail then this results in the highest risk assigned to any of these indicators. Note, this table is based on our own opinion while it is recommended in future to ask several experts to fill out this table and compute the average risk level per entry.

	http	Invalid certificate	Self-signed certificate	CA unknown	Other services
Info	L	M	L	M	X
Shopping	M	H	M	H	X
Banking	H	H	H	H	H
OSN	M	H	M	M	X
E-mail	M	H	H	H	X
Data	M	H	M	M	X
Others	M	M	M	M	X

Table 1: Risk level

The possible (enabling) threat if logging in is for all cases identity theft at this account and if the same password is used for other accounts at these accounts as well. Possible **consequences** are: attacker gets access to private data (e.g. shopping history, salary, photos, and email history), losing money, and different types of nuisance. Note, we will investigate more in the concrete consequences when developing proposals for the content of interventions in future.

Decision prediction. The algorithm needs to take into account the personal characteristics and the user influencing indicators. From the literature it is not possible to predict the decision based on corresponding input data. It is rather likely that experts would verify that https in place when logging in on an e-banking or e-shopping page independent from the design and whether they know the company or not. However, as there is no paper that clearly states this, we recommend conducting a corresponding user study for clarification as future work. For this paper, we assume that everyone would log in on any web page based on the existing passive warnings and if not active warning appears. Thus, it is necessary to support the user with additional security interventions.

6. Intervention strategy

General strategy. While all users need support in detecting potentially critical password transmissions, laypersons also need information about the situation and consequences if deciding to login despite the warning. Thus, we propose to use passive interventions for experts (as this seems to be sufficient in many situations) and active once for laypersons. Note, as such we would also educate users. As the consequence, the number of active interventions can be reduced over time as laypersons learn more and more about the consequences in different situations.

Algorithm description: we propose the following steps:

- Security check (password field and any other security indicator)
  - o If at least one causes a problem continue
- Check history/setup for intention and type
  - o If in history compare whether security decreased
    - ▪ If increased warn
    - ▪ If not reaction according to setting in history
  - o If not continue
- Get web page type from NLP check with corresponding probability
- Get personal characteristics from setup

Afterwards it needs to be decided whether it is necessary to ask the user about his intention and the type of webpage. For experts (CASE 1.E) we propose to use only a passive indicator namely a red background colour for the password field. However, once the user clicks on the password fields and starts entering a password a warning according to the proposal of Maurer *et al.* in (2011a and b) will appear. Note, the content of this active intervention will be different from Maurer et al.'s proposal. For laypersons (CASE 1.L), the tool proceeds in the same manner as for (CASE 1.E) if the result of the NLP check is 'information page' with a high probability.

If the NLP check results for a layperson in one of the other five web page types with a high probability (CASE 2), the user will see a dialog mentioning that there might be a security risk and asking whether the user plans to log in. If he answers yes (CASE 2.YES), the tool displays a warning informing about the concrete risk and consequences when logging in. Note, the consequence will depend on the type of web page. If the user answers no (CASE 2.NO), the background colour of the password field is set to red like in (CASE 1.E) and the tool is set into a `read only' mode (which is not visible to the user) according to Seidel (2012). In this status the user is able to surf at this domain and read and search for information without being disturbed. But when he tries to login, a warning pop-up is displayed at the precise spot of the browser where the data is entered, again, according to the proposal of Maurer *et al.* in (2011a and b). The warning reminds the user of the dialog displayed earlier and inform the user about the risks and consequences if he decides to login. Afterwards he can still decide whether to login. With this third stage we also address the problem of false positives because the second warning would appear very rarely and so, the effect of habituation is avoided.

If the NLP check is not able to deduce the type of web page (CASE 3), lay persons are asked first whether they intent to log in similar to (CASE 2). If the answer is no (CASE 3.NO) the tool will continue as in (CASE 2.N). If the answer is yes (CASE 3.YES), the user is asked in a second dialog on which web page type he tries to login. Next the tool displays the same type of warning as in (CASED 2.YES).

Note, within all dialogs and warnings the user can store the answer in the history for this domain/URL.

7. Conclusions and Future Work

We started operationalizing the Framework fOr Contextualized security Interventions. We focused on password requesting scenarios. According to the framework, we identified security relevant indicators, user influencing indicators and relevant personal characteristics. We further described how these indicators can be deduced from the context and in the setup phase. Afterwards, we proposed an algorithm to identify threats, consequences and the risk as well as a simplified algorithm to predict the user's decision without intervening. Finally, the intervention strategy was proposed.

As future research, we will use FOCI to deduce systematically content for the security interventions. Here, we will take existing literature into account, e.g. Kauer *et al.* (2012) who observed that the wording of warnings should address the personal risk of the user and possible concrete consequences; and Raja *et al.* (2011) who showed that physical mental models helps improving the efficiency and understandability of computer warnings. In a next step, the tool should also provide recommendations how to proceed; e.g. in the situation that users already have an account on this page, need to get access to the data, or even might notice that they use the same password for another security critical web service. In addition, we will have a closer look on those web pages on which the user cannot login on the first page but only on subpages, e.g. after having made selections what to buy. Note, currently, the tool would only be activated once the page with the password field is loaded which makes it according to Gutmann (2011) harder for the tool to convince the user that there is a problem when logging in. Finally, we will integrate learning mechanisms, i.e. that the strategy and content is adopted over time as we expect people to learn how to behave more securely. Afterwards, the proposed algorithm will be implemented as add-on for Firefox and then tested in a lab study and later in a field study.

8. References

Bartsch, S. and Volkamer, M. (2012). "Towards the Systematic Development of Contextualized Security Interventions". In Designing Interactive Secure Systems, BCS HCI 2012, BCS eWiC repository.

Bravo-Lillo, C., Cranor, L.F., Downs, J., Komanduri, S. (2011a)."Bridging the gap in computer security warnings: A mental model approach". IEEE Security and Privacy, pages 18-26.

Bravo-Lillo, C., Cranor, L. F., Downs, J., Komanduri, S., Sleeper, M. (2011b). "Improving computer security dialogs". In Proceedings of the 13th IFIP TC 13 international conference on Human-computer interaction – Volume Part IV, INTERACT'11, pages 18-35. Springer.

Cranor, L. F. (2008). "A framework for reasoning about the human in the loop". In Proceedings of the 1st Conference on Usability, Psychology, and Security, pages 1-15.

Dhamija, R. , Tygar, J. D. , Hearst M. (2006). "Why phishing works". In: Proceedings of the SIGCHI conference on Human Factors in computing systems, pages 581-590. ACM.

Fogg, B. J. , Marshall, J., Laraki, O., Osipovich, A., Varma, C., Fang, N., Paul, J. , Rangnekar, A., Shon, J., Swani P., Treinen, M. (2001).„What makes web sites credible?: a report on a large quantitative study". In Proceedings of SIGCHI conference, pages 61-68. ACM.

Gutmann, P. (2011). "Security and usability fundamentals". http://static.googleusercontent. com/external_content/untrusted_dlcp/research.google.com/de//pubs/archive/32872.pdf (Accessed 02/ 2013).

Kauer, M., Pfeiffer, T., Volkamer, M., Theuerling, H., Bruder, R. (2012). „It is not about the design - it is about the content! Making warnings more efficient by communicating risks appropriately". GI Sicherheit 2012, pages 187-198.

Maurer, M.-E. , De Luca, A, Hussmann, H. (2011a). "Data type based security alert dialogs". In: Proceedings of the 2011 annual conference extended abstracts on Human factors in computing systems, CHI EA '11, pages 2359-2364. ACM.

Maurer, M.-E., De Luca, A., Kempe, S. (2011b). "Using data type based security alert dialogs to raise online security awareness". In: Proceedings of the Seventh Symposium on Usable Privacy and Security, SOUPS '11, pages 2:1-2:13. ACM.

Raja, F., Hawkey, K., Hsu, S., Wang, K.-L., Beznosov, K. (2011). "Promoting a physical security mental model for personal firewall warnings". In annual conference extended abstracts on Human factors in computing systems, pages 1585-1590. ACM.

Sasse, M. A. , Brostoff, S. . Weirich, D. (2001). "Transforming the 'Weakest Link' - a Human/Computer Interaction Approach to Usable and Effective Security". In Technology Journal, Vol. 19, No. 3. pages. 122-131.

Sasse, M. A., Krol, K., Moroz, M.(2012) "Don't work. Can't work? Why it's time to rethink security warnings", 7th Intern. Conf. on Risks & Security of Internet & Systems, pages 1-8.

Schechter, S. E., Dhamija, R., Ozment, A., Fischer, I. (2007). „Emperor's new security indicators: An evaluation of website authentication and the effect of role playing on usability studies". In IEEE Symposium on Security and Privacy.

Seikel, C. (2012), "Categorization of websites according to the risk during usage" Bachelorthesis, Technische Universität Darmstadt.

Sotirakopoulos, A., Hawkey, K., Beznosov, K. (2011)."On the challenges in usable security lab studies: Lessons learned from replicating a study on SSL warnings". In: the Seventh Symposium on Usable Privacy and Security, ACM.

Sunshine, J., Egelman, S., Almuhimedi, H., Atri, N., Cranor, L. F. (2009). "Crying wolf: an empirical study of SSL warning effectiveness". In: Proceedings of the 18th conference on USENIX security symposium, pages 399-416.

West R. (2008). "The psychology of security". Commuication of ACM 51, 4; pages 34-40.

National Password Security Survey: Results

K. Helkala[1] and T.H. Bakås[2]

[1]Norwegian Defence Cyber Academy and Gjøvik University College
[2]Norwegian Centre for Information Security
e-mail: kirsi.helkala@gmail.com, tone@norsis.no

Abstract

Research, especially in the early 21st century, has shown that education is needed to change people's behaviour regarding password generation, management and storage. As our daily routines and duties have become more dependent on electronic services in the last decade, one could think that qualitative education is nowadays given to users. To verify this assumption we conducted a nation-wide, demographic survey in Norway with a sample of 1003 respondents at the age of 18 to 64. The results show that the education or proper guidance seldom is given leading to the outdated users' behavior.

Keywords

Password security, Information security awareness

1. Introduction

Password authentication has existed several decades and it is likely to remain one of the top authentication mechanisms also in the future (Kuhn and Garrison, 2009, Bonneau and Preibusch, 2010). The latest biannual survey on security incidences, data criminality and countermeasures among Norwegian industry conducted by The Security Council of Norwegian Industry (NSR, 2012) reveals that organizations are increasing their usage of information technologies. For example, from 2008 to 2012 the use of mobile phones to receive emails has increased from 54% to 71%, use of social media for internal information exchange from 0% to 16% and for external information exchange from 3% to 39%. All these accounts are password protected.

It is common to think that everybody has knowledge of how to create, store and manage passwords without education. However, research shows the opposite (Horcher and Tejay, 2009, Katz, 2005, Sasse et al., 2001). As the use of the electronic information technologies increases, one could think that basic training is given to children, in-depth education within studies and repetition guidance in accordance with needs of the working environment. This would lead to increasing information security awareness, including password security. We were eager to learn how the situation is in practice and launched a nationwide password survey in Norway. YouGov Norway, a leading Internet based market research institute in the Nordic region (YouGov, 2013), collected the data. The survey was sent to a natural representation of employees at the age of 18 to 64. A total number of 1003 respondents answered the questionnaire.

2. Related Work

As password authentication is an old method, there are plenty of surveys available, such as pure password surveys e.g. (CSID, 2012), information security awareness surveys e.g. (Talib et al., 2010), password policy surveys e.g. (Florêncio and Herley, 2010) or a nation wide security incidences, data criminality and countermeasures surveys e.g. (NSR, 2012).

The results of NSR survey (NSR, 2012) showed that the amount of given education has decreased from 2010 and only four tenth of newly employed have gotten security training. Talib et al. (Talib et al., 2010) executed a survey about information security awareness within home and work environments. As the survey mainly concentrated on users' understanding of security threats, passwords were also included. 45% of the respondents who had not gotten any security awareness training used passwords containing letters, digits and special characters and the passwords were minimum 8 characters long. 61% of the respondents also kept the passwords to themselves.

Florêncio and Herley studied password policies of 75 different websites (Florêncio and Herley, 2010). They found that sites that accept advertising and purchase-sponsored links have a negative correlation with password strength. Shay et al. studied user attitudes after password policy change in Carnegie Mellom University (Shay et al., 2010). The new policy required the minimum of eight characters and at least one character from each character sets: lower case letters, upper case letters, digits and symbols. The passwords were also compared against dictionaries. Results showed that the users found the new policy annoying but believed it to provide better security. The new passwords were created by modifying the old ones and the use of words and names was the most often used password creation strategy.

Hoonakker et al. (Hoonakker et al., 2009) made a password survey from a human factor perspective in a large organization. The results showed that in average a user had nine password accounts, 18% of the respondents used the same password always, 50% reused sometimes, and in average passwords were renewed seven times a year. A password security survey on Symantec Security Response blog (Haley, 2010) found that 44% of the respondents had more than 20 password protected accounts, 45% had few passwords circulating on their accounts and 63% changed their passwords less than once a year. Kumar (Kumar, 2011) studied usability of passwords in practice among students and staff in University at New Delhi. 60% of the respondents had more than six password accounts, 79% reused their passwords and only 30% used different passwords in different accounts. CSID made a demographical survey about password habits of American consumers (CSID, 2012). 61% of the consumers reused their passwords, 54% had less than five passwords, 44% changed their password less than once a year and 21% had experienced a compromise of an online account.

Previously mentioned pure password surveys are very general and do not separate different user groups based on the background information of respondents. They also fail to look at connections. In our study, we have looked at differences between age, gender, occupation and educational groups and identified reasons for behaviour.

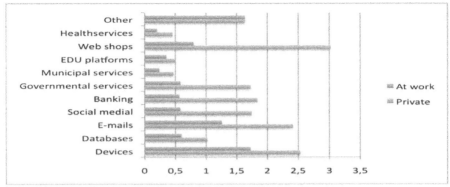

Figure 1: Number of passwords.

3. Results of Questionnaire

We had a total of 1003 respondents. 57% were men, 43% female, 28% were at age 18-34 years, 41% at age 35-49 years and 31% at age 50-64 years. 10% were Executives, 8% Managers, 14% Project managers, 14% Head of departments, 52% Regular employees and 2% were other workers. Questions are listed in Appendix.

3.1. Total numbers of passwords

We found the minimum number of private passwords as 17.3 passwords per person and work related 8.5 passwords per person. *This leads to minimum number of passwords per person to 25.* Figure 1 shows the average number of the password-protected accounts vs. services. The devices included PCs, tablets and phones.

3.2. Education of good passwords

59% of the subjects stated that they had gotten education or guidance on how to generate good passwords. 28% of these had gotten guidelines either from newspapers or websites, 22% at work, 12% during studies and 11% from friends or colleagues. From all respondents, 6% did not remember and *35% stated that they had not gotten any guidance.* This is rather high percentage when considering that password security guidance is often given in security awareness training e.g (Junglemap, 2013). However, the results support a finding in (NSR, 2012) that only four tenths of

	Executive	Manager	Project Manager	Head of Depart.	Regular Employee	Other
Studies	11 %	9 %	16 %	15 %	11 %	6 %
At work	13 %	24 %	39 %	24 %	19 %	0 %
Friends	16 %	16 %	9 %	13 %	10 %	22 %
Websites	**28 %**	**32 %**	**35 %**	**23 %**	**27 %**	**44 %**
Other	3 %	1 %	7 %	1 %	3 %	6 %
Not remem.	7 %	10 %	3 %	8 %	7 %	6 %
Not gotten	**42 %**	**25 %**	**23 %**	**34 %**	**38 %**	**28 %**

Table 1: Password education vs. occupations.

newly employed had gotten training. With 95% confidence, 35±5% of the respondents at age 18-34 years, 35±5% at age 35-49 and 33±5% at age 50-64 had not gotten education meaning that there is no statistical difference between age groups.

Comparison of password education and occupations is shown in Table 1. *Websites and newspapers are the main source of password education. The shocking result was that as high as 42% of executives had not received education.* This might have consequences. Executives have access to most of the assets of the organization. If these assets are password protected, the protection given by the executive might be low. The untrained executives might also oversee the need of education for others.

When asked which websites were used 60% of the respondents did not remember and 1% did not want to say. 10% of those who remembered mentioned VG, 7% Dagbladet and 6% Aftenposten (Norwegian newspapers). 5% of users named The Norwegian Broadcasting Corporation (NRK). Among IT-magazines mostly used was Digi by 12%, ITavisen and Computerword by 1-2% and general information site DinSide by 6% of users. However, none of these sites has a static guidance available. 3% of the respondents listed guidance given by the services themselves. A static

		Password Type (Helkala, 2011)		
		Word	**Mixture**	**Non-Word**
NorSIS (NorSIS, 2012)	**Recommended**	Not mentioned	Yes	Yes
	Min length		20	9
	Character sets		From examples: Uc, lc and sc	From examples: Uc, lc, and d
	Examples		A sentence with a modified letter	First characters from a song
	Other info	Do not reuse, do not share, association helps memorization, change passwords regularly, do not let programs remember passwords and log out after use. Additional information about hacking methods.		
Hardware (Benediktsson, 2012)	**Recommended**	Not	Not mentioned	Yes
	Min length			8, better if 12
	Character sets			Uc, lc, d and sc
	Examples			First characters taken a sentence
	Other info	Avoid using the same character in a password, avoid using characters in the same order that they are found on a keyboard, do not reuse, change regularly. Additional information about hacking methods.		
NSM (NSM, 2002)	**Recommended**	Password type has not been given.		
	Min length	14		
	Character sets	Uc, lc, d and sc		
	Examples	Not given		
	Other info	Do not reuse, change after 90 days, log out, min age for a password one day and if written down, the note has to be stored in a secure place.		

Table 2: Password guidelines by NSM, NorSIS and Hardware.

guidance site is found in IT-magazine Hardware and official security sites of The Norwegian National Security Authority (NSM) and The Norwegian Centre for Information Security (NorSIS), but only 1% of the respondents had found Hardware and 4% NSM and NorSIS. The guidelines are listed in Table 2.

3.3. Description of a good password

After learning where the users got their password guidelines, we were interested to know what they have actually learned. Therefore, we asked them to describe what a good password is in their own words. From all respondents 10% did not want to reveal their description and 4% did not know. The rest 86% had an opinion. We compared those who had gotten guidance and who had not by used character sets and minimum length of passwords, Table 3. *The users with guidance include special characters in their passwords more often than the users without guidance.* There is no statistical difference on the minimum length. However, a good password is more than characters and length. The respondents had considered the following.

Personal information: 19% of the respondents with an opinion considered personal information as worth of mentioning. 35% of these had not gotten guidance and 65% had received guidance. Large majority in *both groups stated that personal information should not be used* and there was no statistical difference between groups (guidance: 95±4% and without guidance: 89±8% with 95% confidence).

Words: 20% of the subjects with an opinion discussed about words. 73% of these had gotten guidance and 27% had not. The use of single words either alone or together with digits, is a bad habit. However, use of several modified words or use of sentences adds robustness against password cracking (Helkala et al. 2012). Due to the small number of users without guidance in this case, we can conclude only with 90% confidence that *the users without guidance more often use pure words* (38±11% of the respondents without guidance and 21±6% with guidance). Modified words where some letters are replaced with other letters, digits or special characters are

		NO GUIDANCE	GUIDANCE
CHARACTER SET	Had no opinion/ Did not want to reveal/ Did not know	38%	19%
	Had an opinion	62% 1 Char set: 1,3% 2 Char sets: 30% 3 Char sets: 56% 4 Char sets: 13±4% (95% conf.)	81% 1 Char set: 0,3% 2 Char sets: 23% 3 Char sets: 54% 4 Char sets: 23±4% (95% conf.)
MIN LENGHT	Had no opinion/ Did not want to reveal/ Did not know	89%	78%
	Mentioned	11% Average: 7,6 ±0,4 (95% conf.)	22% Average: 8,1 ±0,4 (95% conf.)

Table 3: Guidance/No guidance vs. Character sets and length (1 set: digits, 2 sets: digits and one set of letters, 3 sets: digits and both letter cases, 4 sets: all characters.)

used by 2% of the respondents without guidance and 4% with guidance. 53% of the respondents without guidance and 65% with guidance stated that words should not be used. However, the education shows in *variation of password structures*. 8% of the users with guidance gave memorization tricks such as passphrase and 9% use full sentences. For non-educated, the percentages are 0% and 6%, respectively.

Summa summarum, according to majority of respondents "*A good password is a mixture of letters and digits*." This statement is not corresponding to the Norwegian security authorities (NSM, 2009, NorSIS, 2012) or NIST (NIST, 2009). The description is not a surprise taking into account that more than half of the respondents have not had guidance or have received it from websites. The private devices together with web shops, email, social media and cloud accounts constitutes at least half of the private password accounts and when the top traffic sites such as Google, Facebook, Yahoo! and Youtube accept weak passwords as min length between 6-8 characters and only one character sets (Florêncio and Herley, 2010) it is no wonder that a good password description is as it is. When asked if the users follow their own "good password" description 25% of the respondents claimed that all their passwords are good ones, 38% stated that most of them are, 24% said that some of them are good, 8% did not have any good ones and 5% did not know.

As an alternative for own password creation, passwords can be gotten from online password generators e.g. (GRC 2013). However, there is no guarantee that generated passwords are not further used in either direct attacks or indirect attacks by adding hashes of the passwords on online hash lists. The respondents were asked to comment these generators. Results showed that 46% of the respondents had never heard of them and 10% thought that they were good tools for password generation. 13% of the respondents do not use them because they do not know who has access to the generated passwords and 16% do not use them because the generated passwords are hard to remember. 13% did not have an opinion and 3% had some other opinion.

3.4. Confidential Information Protected by Extra Good Passwords

We do not claim that all passwords should be good or strong ones. The accounts that do not contain private and confidential information such as sport activity blogs do not need strong protection. Therefore, we were interested to see how end-users themselves rank the different services based on the accounts' security need, and if they use stronger passwords in these accounts. Figure 2 shows that more than *90% of the respondents stated that bank accounts need to be well protected, more than 70% said the same about email-accounts, and more than 65% considered devices and governmental services* like online social security service as accounts that need stronger password protection. *However, only 31% of the respondents always use stronger passwords in the services they thought should be protected by better passwords*, 27% use usually, 19% sometimes, 19% do not use and 5% do not know.

3.5. Reuse and remembering of Passwords

In our study, *12% of the respondents always reuse their passwords, 62% reuse sometimes* and 15% seldom. 9% of the subjects stated that they never reuse their

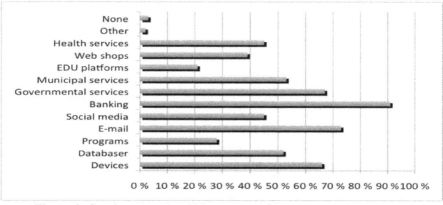

Figure 2: Services that should be protected by extra good passwords

passwords and 2% do not know. The percent of reuse is high. However, there is a difference between genders. We found that *males reuse less passwords than females* ("do not reuse" with 95% confidence: men 12±3% and female 6±2%). There is no statistical difference between ages. Figure 3 shows reuse percentages vs. gender and age. 43% of the respondents claimed to remember all their passwords, 33% use reset option for the passwords their cannot recall, 20% write them down, 1% remember only the login passwords and otherwise trust the browser to remember the rest and 3% use some other methods. We also wanted to know where the passwords are written down. *51% of those who write passwords down have a note either at home or at work place*, 23% store passwords on a text file either on PC or phone, 11% use software for storing, 13% have other methods, 6% carry a note with them and 3% do not know. Differences among genders were found. *With 90% confidence men trust their memory more than females when it comes password remembering and with 95% confidence females more often use a reset option* (remember all passwords: men 46±3% and female: 38±4%, use reset option: men 29±4% and female: 39±5%).

3.6. Sharing Passwords

Among our respondents, *63% do not share their passwords, 31% share with a spouse or partner,* 7% with their children, 4% with colleagues, 2% with IT, 2% with

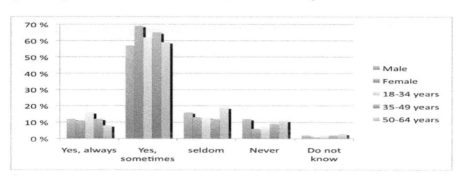

Figure 3: Reuse of passwords among gender and age groups

friends, 1% with bank and 1% with boss. There is no statistical difference between different genders or different age groups. We were also keen on knowing which accounts users trusted for others to use when they shared their passwords. *An interesting finding is that passwords, which protect devices, are earlier stated to be the stronger passwords, however, they are also the most often shared passwords*, see Figure 4. The next shared passwords belong to programs and web shop accounts. The data indicates that females share their private passwords more than males. However, the difference is not statistical significant. It can also be noted that users share their work passwords less than private ones.

4. Conclusion and Future Work

We conducted a nationwide survey of password security with sample of 1003 respondents in Norway. We found that in average a person has minimum of 25 passwords. Not enough qualitative education or guidance is given. Password guidance is left with commercial companies, which are mostly concerned about the easiness of passwords, not the strength of passwords. The good guidelines for passwords given by information security authorities are not among the websites where users search guidance. In the users' opinion the general description of good password is *"A good password is a mixture of letters and digits."* Passwords are very often reused. The users do understand which accounts contain confidential and private information. However, they do not use any better password to protect them. Passwords are shared but mostly with close family members. Even if the password authentication method is old, it is not going to change soon. In order to keep the users updated, we need to invest in education and guidance from the root to top level.

The general results of the password survey have gotten media attention in Norway such as (Thorvaldsen, 2012) and NorSIS had already used the results in national security strategy meetings to wake up governmental departments to realise the real knowledge level of the Norwegian companies and inhabitants. Also meetings with vendors to help them give better password guidance as well as change their policies are to be arranged. NorSIS organizes awareness training amongst Norwegian companies and uses media to reach a bigger population of inhabitants. A national

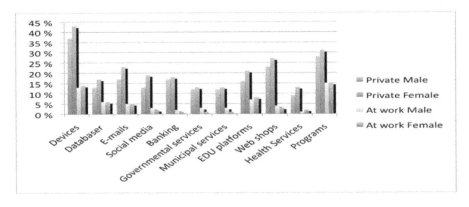

Figure 4: Shared passwords

campaign "The National Security Month" was arranged together with other security experts in October 2012, and a bigger campaign in 2013 is under planning. The campaign will contain commercials in national radio channels, articles in national newspapers and media, awareness training for Norwegian SMEs and speeches for Norwegian companies as charity from Norwegian security experts. The password security will be part of the campaign. The security awareness is also promoted during the year in each of those over a hundred speeches given by NorSIS.

5. References

Benediktsson, A., (2012) "Passordhåndtering", www.hardware.no/artikler/passordhaandtering/78112 (Accessed 8.1.2013)

Bonneau, J. and Preibusch, S. (2010), "The password thicket: technical and market failures in human authentication on the web", In Proc. of WEIS 10

CSID (2012), "Comsumer survey: Password habits, September 2012", www.csid.com/wp-content/uploads/2012/09/ CS_PasswordSurvey_FullReport_FINAL.pdf (Accessed 8.1.2013)

Florêncio, D. and Herley, C. (2010), "Where Do Security Policies Come From?" In Proc. of Symposium on Usable Privacy and Security (SOUPS 2010)

Gibson Research Corporation Web Site (GRC) (2013), "Perfect passwords", www.grc.com/passwords.htm (Accessed 12.1.2013)

Haley, K. (2010), "Symantec - Password Survey Results", www.symantec.com/connect/blogs/password-survey-results (Accessed 8.1.2013)

Helkala, K. (2011), "Password Education Based on Guidelines Tailored to Different Password Categories" Journal of Computers, Vol. 6, Nr 5, Academy Publisher, Finland.

Helkala, K., Svendsen, N.K., Thorsheim, P. and Wiehe, A. (2012), "Cracking Associative Passwords". In Proc. 17th Nordic Conference, NordSec 2012, LNCS Vol.7617, p. 153-168.

Hoonakker, P., Bornoe, N. and Carayon, P. (2009), "Password Authentication from a Human Factors Perspective: Results of a Survey among End-Users", In Proc. of the Human Factors and Ergonomics Society 53rd Annual Meeting, p. 459-463.

Horcher, A.-M. and Tejay, G.P. (2009), "Building A Better Password: The Role of Cognitive Load in Information Security Training", In Proc. of IEEE International Conference on Intelligence and Security Informatics, ISI, p. 113–118.

Junglemap Corporation Web Site, 2013, junglemap.com/ (Accessed 15.1.2013)

Katz, F.H. (2005), "The Effect of a University Information Security Survey on Instruction Methods in Information Security". In Proc. of the Information Security Curriculum Development Conference, p 43–48.

Kuhn, T.B. and Garrison, C. (2009), "A survey of passwords from 2007 to 2009". In 2009 Information Security Curriculum Development Conference, InfoSecCD'09, p. 91–94.

Kumar, N. (2011), "Password in Practice: An usability survey", Journal of Global Research in Computer Science, Vol. 2, No. 5, pp.107-112.

Nasjonal sikkerhetsmyndighet Corporation Web Site (2002), "Veiledning til $ 5-26: Utarbeidelse av brukerinsturks", (Accessed 8.1.2013)

NorSIS , 2012, "Passordvett", www.norsis.no/veiledninger/Passord.html (Accessed 8.1.2013)

NIST Special Publication 800-118 (2009), "Guide to Enterprise Password Management", csrc.nist.gov/publications/drafts/800-118/draft-sp800-118.pdf

Næringslivets sikkerhetsråd (NSR) (2012), "Mørketallsundersøkelse 2012", www.nsr-org.no/getfile.php/Dokumenter/NSR%20publikasjoner/M%C3%B8rketallsunders%C3%B8kel sen/moerketall_2012.pdf

Sasse, M.A., Brostoff, S. and Weirich, D. (2001), "Transforming the "weakest link"-human/ computer interaction approach to usable and effective security", BT Technol,19(19)p.122-131.

Shay, R., Komanduri S., Kelley, P.G., Leon, P.G., Mazurek, M.L., Bauer, L., Christin, N. and Cranor, L.F. (2010), "Encountering Stronger Password Requirements: User Attitudes and Behaviors", In Proc. of the Symposium on Usable Privacy and Security (SOUPS 2010).

Talib, S., Clarke, N.L, and Furnell, S.M.   (2010), "An Analysis of Information Security Awareness within Home and Work Environments", In Proc. of ARES 10, p. 196-203.

Thorvaldsen, L. (2012), "Majoriteten av Norge tror at det vet hva som er et godt passord", dagbladet.no/2012/12/05/nyheter/innenriks/datasikkerhet/passord/24685246/ (Access 20.1.13)

YouGov Corporation Web Site (2013), www.yougov.no/ (Accessed 14.1.2013)

Appendix - Questions

With products/services we mean *devices, cloud services/databases, e-mails, social media, banking, governmental services, municipal services, web shops, health services and other.*

1. How many of the following products and /or services that require a password do you have in your private life and at work? *Product/Services.*
*2.*Have you received guidance for password creation? Where or from who? *While studying; At work; From friends/colleagues; Websites/newspapers; Other; Not remember; Not gotten.*
3. You answered that you received education/guidance from websites/newspapers. Can you specify on which website? *A list of Norwegian sites; Other; Not remember; No.*
4. Describe what you think is a good password and how you create it? (Open).
5. Do your passwords meet your own "good password" description? *All of them; Most of them; Some of them; None of them; Not know.*
6. Which of the following products and/or services provide information that you believe should be kept secret and therefore need extra protection? *Products/Services.*
7. Do you use "better" passwords in the services that you think should be extra protected? *Always; Usually; Sometimes; No; Not know.*
8. Do you reuse your passwords? *Always; Sometimes; Seldom; Never, Not know.*
9. Which of the following statements is best suited to describe how you remember your passwords? *I always remember them; I write them down; I reset them if not remembering; I have checked "remember me" boxes and only remember my login password; Other.*
10. Where do you write passwords down? *On a note I store at home/work; On a note I bring with me; In a text file on my PC/Phone; A computer program for storing; Other; Not know.*
11. What do you think of password generators available on the Internet? *Never heard; A good tool for generating passwords; A scary tool. Do not use them because do not know who has*

access to the generated passwords; Do not use them because generated passwords are hard to remember; Other; Not know.

12. Do you share any of your passwords with any of the following? *Spouse/Partner; Own children; Friends; Colleagues; Boss; Police; Bank; Supplier; IT; Anyone; Do not share.*

13. Do you think it is okay to share any of the following passwords with others, either private and/or work? *Products/Services*

An Analysis of Information Security Vulnerabilities at Three Australian Government Organisations

K. Parsons[1], A. McCormac[1], M. Pattinson[2], M. Butavicius[1], C. Jerram[2]

[1]*Defence Science and Technology Organisation, Edinburgh, Australia*
[2]*Business School, University of Adelaide, Australia*

Abstract

This paper reports on a study conducted by The University of Adelaide with the support of the Defence Science and Technology Organisation, to examine information security (InfoSec) vulnerabilities caused by individuals, and expressed by their knowledge, attitude and behaviour. A total of 203 employees, from three large Australian government organisations, completed a web-based questionnaire designed to capture the knowledge, attitude and behaviour of individuals in regard to InfoSec. In conjunction with this employee questionnaire, qualitative interviews were conducted with a small number of senior management employees from each of the three organisations. Overall, the questionnaire results indicated that employees from all three organisations had reasonable levels of awareness of InfoSec vulnerabilities. Analysis of the qualitative interviews revealed that management not only had an accurate understanding of their employees' InfoSec awareness, but were able to recognise vulnerable areas that required further attention and improvement, such as the appropriate use of wireless technology, the reporting of security incidents and the use of social networking sites.

Keywords

Information security (InfoSec), InfoSec behaviour, Information Risk, InfoSec awareness, InfoSec vulnerabilities

1. Introduction

Management of InfoSec is a critical issue for both public and private sector organisations and there are growing expectations for organisations to ensure a high level of security of electronic data. Historically, problems with InfoSec have demanded a focus on technical solutions such as the development of hardware, software and network solutions. However, InfoSec is not only a technical problem, but is also a 'people' problem (Schultz, 2005). InfoSec-related issues can be better addressed by also considering the influence of the human factor to complement hardware and software solutions (Schneier, 2000).

The aim of this research project was twofold. The first aim was to gain a holistic understanding of the level of InfoSec awareness, defined by the dimensions knowledge, attitude and behaviour, of employees from Australian Government Organisations. The second aim was to develop and test an *Information Security Awareness Instrument* to assess the InfoSec awareness of employees. An inductive, qualitative approach was utilised in the development of the survey tool rather that the more commonly used theory verification approach (Karjalainen, 2011). This meant that questions were developed before a model was applied, thus minimising the effect of bias (Karjalainen, 2011). This process formed the hypothesis that if computer users are in possession of adequate *knowledge* of InfoSec, this should result in a more positive *attitude* towards InfoSec, which should then result in more positive InfoSec *behaviour*. Hence, our three main dimensions of interest are knowledge, attitude and behaviour. This is sometimes referred to as the KAB model and has been studied in fields including InfoSec (Kruger & Kearney, 2006), climate change (van der Linden, 2012) and health promotion (Bettinghaus, 1986).

2. Method

2.1. Participants

Employees of three Australian Government organisations were invited via email to participate in a web-based questionnaire, and their participation was anonymous and voluntary. Response rates varied across the three organisations. In Organisation A, 123 of the 222 invited employees completed the questionnaire, resulting in a response rate of 55%. In Organisation B, 52 of the 200 invited employees completed the questionnaire, resulting in a response rate of approximately 26%. In Organisation C, 28 of the 746 invited employees completed the questionnaire, which equates to a response rate of approximately 4%. Hence, the overall response rate was approximately 17%.

It is important to highlight that the response rate of Organisation C is very low, which greatly affects the ability to generalise the findings. This means that the employees in Organisation C who chose to answer the questionnaire are likely to be systematically different from other employees of that organisation, and are essentially self-selected (Fowler, 2002). Fowler (2002) claims that self-selected participants in small sample sizes are more likely to have an interest in the topic in question. This means that the actual level of InfoSec awareness in Organisation C is likely to be lower than the level estimated by our study.

2.2. Web-based Questionnaire

The questionnaire was designed around eight aspects of InfoSec management:

- *Importance of InfoSec policies,*
- *Principles of InfoSec policies,*
- *Rules of InfoSec policies,*
- *Password management,*
- *Email and internet usage,*
- *Reporting security incidents,*
- *Consequences of behaviour* and *Training.*

These focus areas were chosen such that they allowed the researcher to identify any specific InfoSec weaknesses that could be subsequently addressed by management in the form of training, communication and policy development.

Participants were asked questions about their understanding of InfoSec threats and their experiences with InfoSec training within their organisation. More broadly, participants were asked to provide details about their general computer practices. Responses were used to produce measures of each of the eight focus areas along one or more of the dimensions: knowledge, attitude and behaviour.

Self-report questionnaires are often influenced by response bias and social desirability bias. Response pattern bias is observed when participants select the same response to every question. In order to eliminate and detect this behaviour, negatively worded questions were purposefully included in the questionnaire design. Social desirability bias is observed when individuals respond in a way that ensures they are seen to be behaving appropriately (Edwards, 1953). This bias, and the possible effects on results, is examined in more detail in the Discussion of this paper.

2.3. Management Interviews

To complement the questionnaire, qualitative interviews were conducted with members of senior management from each organisation. Three interviews were conducted with Organisation A, three interviews with Organisation B and two interviews with Organisation C. Each interview was conducted by two researchers with one member of senior management.

3. Results

3.1. Overview

Overall, the InfoSec awareness of employees who responded to the questionnaire was high. As mentioned previously, employee InfoSec awareness was assessed using three dimensions, namely, knowledge, attitude and behaviour. To provide more in-depth context specific information, the dimensions were divided into eight focus areas.

A number of questions were administered to provide a measure of each of these components, and Table 1 shows a summary of the results for each of the organisations. The mean score is shown with the standard deviation in brackets. Values range from '0' to '1' where '0' represents the least appropriate response and '1' the most desirable. Sample questions and results are also shown in Appendix A.

	Components	Organisation A	Organisation B	Organisation C	Total
Dimensions	Knowledge	0.92 (0.08)	0.86 (0.12)	0.91 (0.07)	0.90 (0.09)
	Attitude	0.86 (0.08)	0.76 (0.13)	0.86 (0.21)	0.83 (0.13)
	Behaviour	0.85 (0.08)	0.79 (0.09)	0.80 (0.09)	0.83 (0.09)
Focus Area	Importance of InfoSec policy	0.91 (0.09)	0.85 (0.16)	0.91 (0.22)	0.90 (0.13)
	Rules of InfoSec policy	0.87(0.08)	0.81 (0.10)	0.86 (0.13)	0.85 (0.10)
	Principles of InfoSec policy	0.92 (0.09)	0.85 (0.17)	0.90 (0.23)	0.90 (0.14)
	Password management	0.92 (0.10)	0.86 (0.12)	0.82 (0.11)	0.89 (0.11)
	Email and internet usage	0.88 (0.07)	0.83 (0.10)	0.90 (0.10)	0.87 (0.09)
	Report security incidents	0.71 (0.20)	0.65 (0.21)	0.70 (0.25)	0.69 (0.21)
	Consequences of behaviour	0.83 (0.12)	0.69 (0.16)	0.81 (0.21)	0.76 (0.16)
	Training	0.82 (0.14)	0.68 (0.16)	0.81 (0.26)	0.78 (0.17)

Table 1: Summary Results

It is important to highlight that this measure is still undergoing development, and has been completed by only 203 participants, who were not necessarily representative of the whole organisation. Hence, any comparisons between the organisations should be interpreted cautiously. For this reason, this report will only describe overall comparisons, based on the major dimensions of InfoSec awareness.

3.2. InfoSec Knowledge

In the section designed to capture knowledge about InfoSec, employees were provided with 15 statements. The purpose of these statements was to ascertain the employees' level of understanding of a number of important InfoSec rules. These statements addressed security considerations such as password selection, email and social networking site use, and using wireless technology to access information.

Participants could respond to each statement with either 'True', 'False' or 'Unsure', and the responses to each statement were assigned values from one to three. This assignment was such that, the more appropriate the response, the higher the value assigned to it, and a response of 'Unsure' was assigned a value of two (which is the middle value). Hence, for reverse questions, the scores were inverted, so that a higher score always corresponds with a better or more appropriate response.

The average scores were very high for the majority of the statements. All three organisations obtained average scores of 90% or higher for seven of the knowledge-based statements, and 80% or higher for a further six statements. This means that most employees had an appropriate knowledge of InfoSec. Results indicate that respondents had a good understanding of the importance of InfoSec rules, and had an accurate knowledge of password security, and recognised that passwords should not consist solely of real words or significant dates or names.

Employees' knowledge of the security of wireless technologies was less convincing. As depicted in Appendix A, in response to the statement *"Wireless computing is considered to be less secure than wired computing"* the average score obtained by Organisation A was only 67%, and Organisations B and C had average scores of only 60% and 55%, respectively. Since wireless computing can pose a potential security risk, this is an area where education may be required.

In summary, the InfoSec knowledge demonstrated by respondents from Organisations A and C tended to be slightly higher than the knowledge demonstrated by Organisation B. However, this was usually only a difference of a few percentage points.

3.3. InfoSec Attitude

In the section assessing attitude towards InfoSec, employees were asked *"In terms of your work environment, how strongly do you agree with the following statements"*. Employees were asked to respond to 20 statements on a five-point scale from 'Strongly Disagree' to 'Strongly Agree'. The statements addressed areas such as the importance of InfoSec within their organisation, their exposure to training and their understanding of their responsibilities for maintaining InfoSec.

Employees' responses to each statement were assigned values from one to five. This assignment was such that, the more appropriate the response, the higher the value assigned to it. Hence, for reverse questions, the scores were inverted, so that a higher score always corresponds with a better or more appropriate response.

Employees of all organisations were judged to have a reasonable attitude towards InfoSec, with average scores for most variables at over 60%. The vast majority of employees from all three organisations recognised that their organisation has information that needs to be protected, believed that InfoSec is an important issue in their organisation, and recognised that it is important for them to act securely in all aspects of their work.

Generally speaking, employees from Organisations A and C were more likely to provide the most appropriate response than the employees from Organisation B. The largest difference between the organisations was obtained in response to the statement *"I believe that adequate security training is provided"*. Most participants from Organisation A and C agreed with this statement, with average scores of 75% and 78% respectively. In contrast, the average score obtained for Organisation B for this statement was only 49%.

There was also a large variation in response to the statement *"What I do on social networking sites is none of my employer's business"*. The vast majority of employees from Organisation C recognised that their behaviour on these sites is of some interest to their employer, with an average score of 79%, whereas the average scores provided by Organisations A and B were only 58% and 59%, respectively. Since social networking sites can have numerous negative consequences, such as jeopardising the security, confidentiality and reputation of an organisation (Parsons, McCormac & Butavicius, 2011), this is therefore an area where education may be required for employees from Organisations A and B.

3.4. InfoSec Behaviour

In the section assessing InfoSec behaviour, participants were provided with 16 statements and were asked to indicate how frequently they engaged in certain behaviours, both conducive and detrimental to InfoSec. Examples include, *"I delete suspicious emails"*, *"I share my password with others"*, and *"I open attachments from unknown sources"*. Participants were asked to respond on a five-point scale, from 'Never' to 'Always', and the responses to each statement were assigned values from one to five. This assignment was such that, the more appropriate the response, the higher the value assigned to it.

In summary, self-reported behaviour of employees from all organisations was considered reasonable, with an average score for most questions of 70% or higher. Although there was some variation across the questions, generally speaking, the respondents from Organisation A were most likely to respond appropriately, and the employees from Organisation B were less likely to do so.

The vast majority of employees from all organisations reported that they never share their passwords with others, and would never download non-corporate software or music or video content from the Internet onto their work computers. Although most employees from Organisation A would not use a USB stick to transfer files between work and home, a number of employees from Organisations B and C admitted that they sometimes do so.

Results also indicated that many people do not keep a clear and tidy desk at work, and there were also areas associated with reporting of security incidents where people did not respond appropriately. For example, in response to the statement *"If I see unfamiliar people in my office area I will approach them and ask to see their identification,"* employees from Organisation A scored an average of 56%, Organisation B scored an average of 49% and Organisation C scored an average of 69%. The response to this statement must be examined in light of the organisation in question. Some organisations have a policy where visitors must be escorted, and therefore, it is not appropriate for someone to approach an escorted visitor, but it would be necessary to approach an unfamiliar person if the individual in question is not being escorted.

3.5. Management Interviews

To determine whether management within the three organisations had a good understanding of the InfoSec awareness of their employees, members of senior management from each organisation were interviewed. A total of eight interviews were carried out. Although the interviewees all held senior management positions within their organisations, some were responsible for day-to-day operations and people management, whereas others were specifically responsible for InfoSec management.

A semi-structured interview technique was utilised, and the interviews included questions regarding InfoSec policy, procedures, culture and management attitude towards InfoSec.

Generally, the information provided by the senior managers of all three organisations was consistent with the responses from the employees of their organisations, indicating that management have a good understanding of the InfoSec awareness of their employees. Essentially, management believed that most employees have an appropriate level of InfoSec awareness, but recognised that there were areas of improvement required.

The managers had a very good knowledge not only of the InfoSec policies of their organisation, but also understood what constituted good InfoSec management in general. The managers recognised that there can be tensions between the necessity to abide by any security regulations and the need to get the job done. They also explained that there can be challenges associated with keeping any InfoSec policy current with so many fast changing technological advances.

However, the managers believed that most employees have a sense of responsibility and professionalism for the information held by their organisation. Therefore, managers believed that security breaches would be more likely to be caused by unintentional lapses rather than maliciousness. Managers believe that this was particularly true of employees who had been with the organisation for some time, as this sense of responsibility and professionalism is stronger once employees have been enculturated within the organisation. With new employees, the managers of all organisations explained that a greater emphasis is placed on punitive measures.

All managers also acknowledged that their organisation has potential vulnerabilities associated with the use of social networking sites, and although the potential risks associated with these sites should be covered by current policies associated with Internet usage and general privacy or confidentiality rules, the managers still acknowledged that this is an area where further education is required to emphasise the possible risks, and reinforce the restrictions on use.

In summary, the results of the management interviews support the findings from the employee questionnaires. Essentially, managers recognised that there were some weaknesses with regards to InfoSec awareness, training and compliance, but generally believed that most employees at their organisation have a reasonable level of InfoSec awareness.

4. Discussion

Interviews were conducted with members of senior management from three organisations, and employees of these organisations were asked to complete a web-based questionnaire, which contained questions relating to demographic details, perceived information risks, knowledge of information security policies, information security attitudes, and behaviour whilst using a computer.

The results of this survey indicate that the level of awareness of employees within all three organisations was generally satisfactory. Overall, answers to questions relating to knowledge received higher scores than those for attitude and behaviour. A summary of the most important findings is provided below:

- The InfoSec knowledge of employees was very good. Employees from all organisations scored 90% or higher in response to seven knowledge-based statements, and 80% or higher in response to a further six statements. Respondents had a good understanding of the importance of InfoSec rules, and had an accurate knowledge of password security, and recognised that passwords should not contain only real words or significant dates or names. There were, however, some aspects of wireless technology where many employees lacked knowledge.

- Most respondents also had a good attitude towards InfoSec. However, in general, the scores for their attitude-based questions were slightly lower than those based on their knowledge. Employees generally recognised that their organisation has information that needs to be protected, believed that InfoSec is an important issue in their organisation, and recognised that it is important for them to act securely in all aspects of their work. However, responses indicated that Organisation B may need to improve their InfoSec training, and all organisations may need to educate employees about the use of social networking sites.

- Reported employee behaviour was also good. Overall, scores for the behaviour-based questions were similar to those testing their attitude. Most employees stated that they would never share their passwords with others, and would never download non-corporate software or music or video content from the Internet onto their work computers. However, people were far less likely to keep a clear and tidy desk, and there were areas associated with the reporting of security incidents where people did not respond appropriately. In addition, while most employees from Organisation A knew not to use a USB stick (thumb drive) to transfer files between work and home, a number of employees from Organisations B and C admitted that they sometimes do so.

- Interviews with senior management revealed that the managers had a good understanding of the InfoSec awareness of their employees, and understood what constituted good InfoSec management in general. However, they also acknowledged some areas of concern such as the need for more education in the appropriate use of social networking sites whilst at work.

It is important to highlight that the data from Organisation C is based on only 28 employees due to a very poor response rate. It is likely that those who chose to respond are systematically different from the employees who did not participate in the questionnaire which greatly affects the generalisability of the findings from this organisation.

There are a number of possible limitations associated with this research. For example, the results of this report are based on self-report which does not always reflect true attitudes and behaviour, as some respondents may be influenced by biases. For example, according to the social desirability bias, respondents may consciously or unconsciously answer in a way that ensures that they are presented in a positive light (Edwards, 1953). However, previous research has shown that an individual's perceptions, attitudes and knowledge can be appropriately measured via self-report (Schmitt, 1994; Spector, 1994). Additionally, to further decrease the influence of this bias, and increase the chance that employees responded openly about InfoSec awareness, employees were informed that the survey was being conducted anonymously.

5. Conclusions and Future Research

In general, participants scored slightly higher on questions testing their knowledge than for those regarding behaviour and attitude. While it is difficult to compare scores directly across these three areas, this finding is nonetheless consistent with the sentiment echoed by the managers in their interviews; namely, that employees generally possessed good knowledge of InfoSec even if their actions were not always consistent with good policy. This suggests that any remedial action might be best directed towards training programs to improve policy compliance that focus on changing the behaviour of participants. This training should be contextualised (i.e., tailored to the specific needs of the audience) and use case studies (Brooke, 2006) rather than generic courses that resemble lectures in order to improve compliance with, rather than simply knowledge of, policy (Parsons, McCormac, Butavicius, & Ferguson, 2010). In particular, as evidenced with both questionnaire participants and management interviewees, the use of social networking sites is still a potential issue and specialised training programs may be beneficial (Parsons et al., 2011).

The next stage of research will examine the effectiveness of various training and risk communication options by using the questionnaire developed in this current research in a pre-test/post-test methodology. For example, the authors are interested in developing e-simulation scenarios and comparing the effectiveness of this form of training with more traditional methods such as lectures. Furthermore, the authors intend to refine the questionnaire presented in this report so that it can be used as the basis of benchmarking the state of information security within various industries. The questionnaire could also be used to track the long-term InfoSec health of an organisation over a significant period of time (Wilson & Hash, 2003).

6. References

Bettinghaus, E. P. (1986), "Health promotion and the knowledge-attitude-behavior continuum", *Preventive Medicine*, Vol. 15, No. 5, pp475-491.

Brooke, S. L. (2006), "Using the case method to teach online classes: Promoting Socratic dialogue and critical thinking skills", *International Journal of Teaching and Learning in Higher Education*, Vol. 18, No. 2, pp142-149.

Edwards, A. L. (1953), "The relationship between the judged desirability of a trait and the probability that the trait will be endorsed", *Journal of Applied Psychology*, Vol. 37, No. 2, pp90-93.

Fowler, F. J. (2002), *Survey Research Methods (3rd ed.)*, Sage, Thousand Oaks, CA, ISBN: 1412958415

Karjalainen, M. (2011), *Improving Employees' Information Systems (IS) Security Behaviour: Toward a Meta-Theory of IS Security Training and a New Framework for Understanding Employees' IS Security Behaviour*, PhD, University of Oulu, Oulu. (A 579)

Kruger, H., & Kearney, W. (2006), "A prototype for assessing information security awareness", *Computers & Security*, Vol. 25, No. 4, pp289-296.

Parsons, K., McCormac, A., & Butavicius, M. (2011), *Don't Judge a (Face) Book by its Cover: A critical review of the implications of social networking sites*, Defence Science & Technology Organisation, DSTO-TR-2549.

Parsons, K., McCormac, A., Butavicius, M., & Ferguson, L. (2010), *Human Factors and Information Security: Individual, Culture and Security Environment*, Defence Science and Technology Organisation, DSTO-TR-2484.

Schneier, B. (2000), *Secrets and lies: digital security in a networked world*: Wiley, ISBN: 0-471-25311-1.

Schmitt, N. (1994), 'Method bias: The importance of theory and measurement', *Journal of Organizational Behavior*, Vol. 15, pp393-398

Schultz, E. (2005), 'The human factor in security', *Computers & Security*, Vol. 24, No. 6, pp425-426.

Spector, P.E. (1994), 'Using self-report questionnaires in OB research: A comment on the use of a controversial method', *Journal of Organizational Behavior*, Vol. 15, p385-392.

van der Linden, S. (2012, July), Understanding and achieving behavioural change: Towards a new model for communicating information about climate change. Paper presented at the *International Workshop on Psychological and Behavioural Approaches to Understanding and Governing Sustainable Tourism Mobility*, Freiburg, Germany.

Wilson, M. & Hash, J. (2003), *Computer Security: Building an Information Technology Awareness and Training Program*, NIST SP: 800-50.

Appendix A

Please indicate whether these statements are true or false.

	True	False	Unsure
Wireless computing is considered to be less secure than wired computing	○	○	○

In terms of your work environment, how strongly do you agree with the following statements?

	Strongly Disagree	Disagree	Neither Agree nor Disagree	Agree	Strongly Agree
I believe that adequate security training is provided	○	○	○	○	○
What I do on social networking sites is none of my employer's business	○	○	○	○	○

Please indicate how frequently the following statements apply to you when you are at work.

	Never 1	2	3	4	Always 5
I share my password with others	○	○	○	○	○
If I see unfamiliar people in my office area I will approach them and ask to see their identification	○	○	○	○	○
I open attachments from unknown sources	○	○	○	○	○

Figure A: Screenshot of sample questions as shown to participants

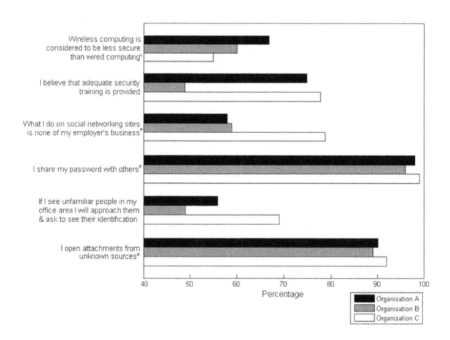

Figure B: Results of sample questions for each organisation

Establishment of Security Knowledge Sharing in Organisations: An Empirical Study

W.R. Flores

Department of Industrial Information and Control Systems, Royal Institute of
Technology, Stockholm, Sweden
e-mail: waldorf@ics.kth.se

Abstract

The purpose of the present study is to empirically investigate what drives the establishment of
security knowledge sharing in organisations. Based on a theoretical understanding a research
model was developed and tested by collecting and analysing data from 62 security executives
from a diverse set of organisations located in different geographic regions in the world. The
empirical tests of a structural model revealed that all proposed hypotheses are accepted, except
the hypotheses proposing a positive link between business-based information security and the
establishment of security knowledge sharing. Organisational structure has a major direct
influence on the establishment of security knowledge sharing in organisations, while the effect
of coordinating information security process is moderate. A mediation analysis revealed that
the reason for the nonsignificant direct relation between business-based information security
and security knowledge sharing is the fully mediating effect of coordinating information
security process. Thus, coordinating information security process has an important role on
security knowledge sharing by either partially or fully mediating the effects of both
organisational structure and business-based information security on security knowledge
sharing. Implications and recommendation for future research are further discussed.

Keywords

Information security, knowledge sharing, partial least squares structural equation
modelling

1. Introduction

The increased dependence and use of IT products and services has forced
organisations to manage risks and ensure information security related to those
products and services. Organisations often try to ensure information security by
establishing a security infrastructure based on technological solutions. These
solutions are useful, and their effectiveness and robustness has made it more difficult
to successfully attack computer systems using purely technical means. Many
attackers have therefore started to include social means in their malicious efforts and
target the humans accessing and using IT products and services (Applegate 2009).
The danger of focusing exclusively on technological solutions and the presence of
new ways to compromise information security has moved the attention to a more
holistic approach to information security, comprising of both technological and
social factors (Kayworth & Whitten 2010). Such a socio-technical approach
emphasizes the importance of taking account of the human element in establishing
information security in an organisation. The understanding of how to manage various

elements of information security is however limited (Dhillon & Backhouse 2001) and empirically research on organisational drivers for the establishment of information security components is even more under-investigated. Factors that are discussed in the extant literature is usually assumed to have an impact on different information security components independently of each other (ISACA 2006; Kayworth & Whitten 2010). As a consequence there is a need to consider research that investigates how to govern and manage dimension of information security in general and socio-organisational dimensions of information security in particular.

Awareness of risks with IT usage, and knowledge on how to prevent, detect and react to security breaches are important facets of a social approach to information security (Dontamsetti & Naranayan 2009; Applegate 2009). In order to increase employee security knowledge, organisations establish different social mechanisms (Kayworth & Whitten 2010). These mechanisms can be manifested through processes of capturing and transferring knowledge of information security, such as establishing security awareness programs, conducting security exercises and implementing IT-based knowledge sharing solutions (Rocha Flores & Ekstedt 2012). The establishment of security knowledge sharing arrangements in a firm depends on how information security is organised and structured. In line with this premise, its logical to argue that it is important to understand determinants of the establishment of information security knowledge sharing in firms. The purpose of the study is therefore to obtain a deeper understanding of how firms structure and organise themselves to enable sharing of information security knowledge to organisational members. In line with the purpose of the study, the following research question was formulated:

Which determinants have a major influence on the establishment of security knowledge sharing in organisations?

In an attempt to answer the research question, data from 62 information security executives from a diverse set of organisations was collected and analysed. The rest of the paper is structured as follows. In the following section, theory is outlined and the hypotheses are developed. The section that follows presents the methodology used to conduct the research. The data is then analysed and presented. Finally, the paper ends with the results being discussed and conclusions being drawn.

2. Theory and Hypothesis Development

2.1 Security Knowledge Sharing

As the focus of information security has shifted from the use of technology-based resources to more tacit resources, human knowledge sharing has emerged as an important factor to manage IT-related risks. In general, knowledge sharing has three dimensions: generation of knowledge, codification of knowledge and transferring of knowledge. In an organisational context, knowledge can either be generated by acquiring or developing it within the organisation (Davenport & Prusak 1998). Thus, organisations can hire information security specialists to perform activities that increase knowledge of information security, or have dedicated units within the organisation that are responsible for those activities. Codification of knowledge refers to the process of making knowledge accessible to those who need it. Companies can save and renew important information security knowledge onto computers for easy browsing and use an intranet site to make information on work task-related risks accessible. Knowledge is transferred when people interact with each other by sharing experience or helping one another. Information security personnel can, for instance, engage in boundary-spanning activities to improve security knowledge sharing among organisational constituents (Kayworth & Whitten 2010). Companies can also provide informal consulting and advisory services to other areas of the company, provide workshops, exercises and training to transfer knowledge (Davenport & Prusak 1998). In the present study security knowledge sharing is conceptualized in two dimensions; formal knowledge sharing arrangements and support for knowledge transfer. Thus, this study aims at understanding what leads firms to establish those two dimensions of knowledge sharing.

2.2 Determinants of Security Knowledge Sharing

The effectiveness of organisational knowledge sharing is influenced by key organisational factors such as structure, processes and strategy (Rhodes et al. 2008). These factors are now described more thoroughly. The descriptions provide the basis for the development of hypotheses linking organisational determinants to the establishment of security knowledge sharing.

Processes to coordinate information security support the integration of information security in key organisational business processes or services and enable security to be a core element in the business environment and thereby strengthen the link between high-level business requirements and operational security procedures (Kayworth & Whitten 2010). In order to coordinate any information security activities, it is first imperative to assess the need for security by identifying vulnerabilities that can negatively affect business operations (Calder & Watkins 2008). Identifying security vulnerabilities in an organisation provides an understanding of risks that need to be mitigated for the protection of its information resources help management make informed information security-related decisions (Sun et al. 2006). In order to coordinate information security, controls need to be checked for their effectiveness in practice. It is therefore imperative that organisations continually receive information on any changes in its business environment that might pose a risk to their information systems (Sun et al. 2006). Establishing performance monitoring ensures that the proper security controls are in place and adapted to the needs of the recipients. Thus, it is a logical deduction to believe that coordinating information security processes influence the establishment of knowledge sharing activities in an organisation. Therefore, the following hypothesis is proposed:

H1: Coordinating information security processes is positively associated with the organisation's establishment of security knowledge sharing.

The information security strategy need to be aligned with the business strategy to ensure that information security is based on actual business needs and not hinders the business from conducting their strategic and operational activities (Kayworth & Whitten 2010). Thus, it is crucial to balance the need to enable the business against the need to secure information assets. Aligning any security activities to business needs is a prerequisite for effective security. Strategic alignment is manifested if a firm's departments act on the firm's business strategy by outlining strategies, plans, and investments that are based on an understanding and knowledge of the business objectives, value, or needs (Henderson & Venkatraman 1993). A deep understanding of the business environments, processes and the organisational goals enables the development of effective IS strategies, provides information services that fit organisational needs and enable IT workforce to conduct proper risk assessments Firms with business competent security executives conduct proper management of information assets and effective allocation of resources (Chang & Wang 2010). Therefore, this paper explores the role of security executives with an understanding of organisational business goals and needs on an organisation's coordinating information security and establishment of security knowledge sharing. This state is referred as business-based information security, and the following two hypotheses are proposed:

H2a: Business-based information security is positively associated with the organisation's coordinating information security processes.

H2b: Business-based information security is positively associated with the organisation's establishment of security knowledge sharing.

Successful companies generally attribute a significant part of their success to good organisation. The design of organisations is therefore one of management's major priorities (Child 1984). Structure has a central role to the design of an effective organisation. Structure is defined as means for attaining the objectives and goals for an organisation (Drucker 1974). In an information security context, structure enables effective organisation of information security and contributes to the successful implementation of information security plans. Further, structure supports the assignment of both technical and human resources to the tasks which have to be done and provide mechanisms for their coordination. Structure also establishes and enables strategic- and operational decision-making and monitoring of performance, and also operating mechanisms that transfers directives on what is expected of organisational members and how the directives can be followed (Child 1984). In this study, organisational structure is manifested through formal structure such as the existence of an organizational unit with explicit responsibility for organizing and coordinating information security, and coordinating structures such as the existence of responsible functions (e.g. senior-level information security executives), and a constitution of a diversity of coordinating security committees and teams that meet to discuss important security issues both formally and informally (Kayworth and Whitten 2010). To understand the impact of organisational structure in the context of information security, the following hypotheses are postulated:

H3a: Organisational structure is positively associated with the establishment of the organisation's security knowledge sharing.

H3b: Organisational structure is positively associated with the organisation's coordinating information security processes.

H3c: Organisational structure is positively associated with the organisation's business-based information security.

The proposed research hypotheses are summarized in figure 1. The interested reader can find further details on the definitions of the investigated constructs and how they were conceptualized in Rocha Flores & Korman (2012).

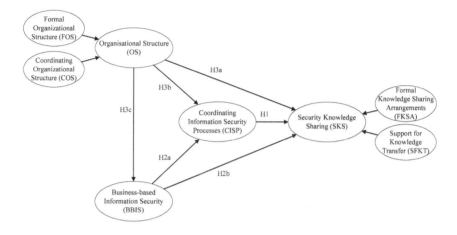

Figure 1: Research model

3. Research Methodology

Due to the challenges in collecting empirical data in the critical domain of information security (Kotulic & Clark 2004), we used the survey method to test our proposed research model.

3.1 Item Development and Content Validity Assessment

The survey items were based on two previous studies; an inductive study with six information security specialists (Rocha Flores & Ekstedt 2012), and a conceptualization of constructs in which an assessment of dimension comprehensiveness and relevance with empirical data from 18 content domain experts was conducted (Rocha Flores & Korman 2012). Security knowledge sharing and organisational structure were operationalised as formative second-order constructs composed of two reflective first-order constructs each: formal knowledge sharing arrangements (FKSA) and support for knowledge transfer (SFKT) represented security knowledge sharing; and formal organisational structure (OS) and coordinating organisational structure (COS) represented organisational structure. These constructions are referred to as a type II second-order construct models (Jarvis et al. 2003). Coordinating information security processes (CISP) was specified with formative items, and the other five first-order construct were specified with reflective multiple items. When possible, the items were based on existing scales that have been proven reliable. Items representing business-based information security (BBIS), were identified from previous work (Chang & Wang 2010; Spears & Barki 2010). Thus, a major part of the items were developed specifically for this study. When developing new items, MacKenzie et al. (2011) recommends to assess the content validity of the items before colleting primary data. Therefore, we first quantitatively assessed the content validity using the item-sorting method proposed by Anderson & Gerbing (1991). This was done for all constructs except BBIS, by obtaining data from 56 content domain experts. We also asked for comments on wording and if the survey items were clearly understood and if they perceived that any items were missing to represent the construct. Based on this pre-test the survey instrument was revised and the initial item pool of containing 34 newly developed items was reduced to 18 items with an adequate degree of content validity. We however decided to exclude two more items for further analysis as they could not be answered by our intended sample without a potential problem associated with common method bias (P. M. Podsakoff et al. 2003). By adding four, already tested and reliable, items representing BBIS, the final survey included 20 items (Cf. Appendix), all measured on a 11-point licker scale from 0 to 10 inspired by Paternoster & Simpson (1996) and Siponen & Vance (2010).

3.2 Primary Data Collection

The SANS security mailing list (GPWN-list), was initially adopted as a sampling frame. The mailing list comprises security executives, senior managers, and managers with operational responsibilities and other practitioners with an interest in information security such as security analysts, security architects and pen-testers. To choose potential respondents, the key informant methodology was used. The key informant methodology advocates that respondents should be identified based on their position, experience, and professional knowledge rather than by the traditional random sampling procedure (Segars & Grover 1999). In our study, the key informants included such high-level executives as CISOs, Security Officers, CEOs, CIOs, and IT managers. From this sampling frame, we identified 548 potential respondents. We also approached security executives from 10 organisations that were known to the research department and asked them to complete the survey. In total, the sample therefore included 558 potential respondents. Data was collected in November and December of 2012. The survey was hosted by a widely used internet-based application (SurveyMonkey). Two reminders were sent to non-responding participants after a first week and a third week in order to increase the response rate. Out of 558 e-mail requests that where sent, 38 bounced or were unregistered from the mailing list. After two reminders 85 had opened the survey and 62 respondents had completed the survey, which gives an effective response rate of 11.1 %. At first glance, the response rate may seem rather low. However, Rogelberg & Stanton (2007) argue that the response rate alone is an inaccurate and unreliable proxy for study quality. The response rate in this study is understandable given that data is collected in the critical domain of information security and that managers have been oversurveyed due to the increased popularity of using online surveys to capture organisational managers' attitudes and beliefs related to different types of organisational issues (Rogelberg & Stanton 2007).

To address potential nonresponse bias the last respondent method was used as recommended by (Armstrong & Overton 1977) and used in Bulgurcu et al. (2010). The method assumes that non-respondents are like the projected last respondent in the last wave of data collection (final reminder). The dataset was split in three groups and a series of independent t-tests was conducted to identify any significant differences in means between the first and the last third of the respondents' data. This test procedure revealed no significant differences between the first and the last third of the respondents' data on any of the items analysed. This suggests that nonresponse bias was not an issue in this study.

The respondents in the sample represent a diverse set of industries and their organisation represents diverse industry groups. Twenty-nine percent of the responding organisations are in IT industries; 16 percent are in the government and academic sector; 15 percent in manufacturing and retail; 11 percent are in financial services and insurance industries; 11 percent are in telecommunication services; 5 percent in Energy; 5 percent in Health care; and 8 percent were categorised as "other". A significant part of the organisations were located in the United States (41.9 percent), Sweden (16.1 percent), Finland (8.1 percent) and United Kingdom (4.8 percent). However, we also received answer from Japan, Egypt, Bermuda, Israel and Turkey. 40 percent of the organisations had more than 500 employees; 19 percent had less than 100 employees; 14 percent between 1000-5000 employees; 14 percent between 100-499; and 12 percent 500-999 employees. A significant number (71 percent) of the respondents are senior executives with job titles such as CISOs, CSOS, CIOs, CEOs, and IT managers. Other titles that the respondents reported to have are; Director of information security, Head of cyber defence section, Information security manager, Cyber security manager, Head of sub-division and Business manager of Critical Infrastructure & industrial security. Further, 87 percent had work with information security within an organisation for 10 or more years.

4. Data Analysis and Results

Partial least squares structural equation modelling (PLS-SEM) was used to test the measurement model's psychometric properties and structural model. PLS-SEM was used instead of covariance-based techniques due to the sample size, the including of a formative construct in the model, and that the focus of the study is to explain variance of the included endogenous variables (Hair et al. 2011). The data set was first screened to identify any outliers as recommended by Hair et al. (2011). This process yielded the identification of four outliers, which were removed for further analysis. We then turned to using SmartPLS the software package (version 2.0.M3)(C.M. Ringle et al. 2005) for the estimations.

4.1 Quality of Measurement Model

Construct validity for the formative construct (CISP) was assessed by examining indicator weights and signs of multicollinearity. Formative measures should not be highly correlated and the variance of a formative indicator should not be explained by the other constructs' indicators. A variance inflation factor less than 5 indicates acceptable shared variance (Hair et al. 2011). One of the formative items indicated to cause correlation (VIF > 5), and was therefore removed for further analysis. As table 1 shows, the remaining formative items had significant weights and acceptable VIFs (* at $p < 0.05$; and ** at $p < 0.01$).

Indicator	VIF	Outer weights
CISP1	1,723	0,478**
CISP2	2,415	0,280*
CISP4	2,068	0,398**

Table 1: Formative construct validity for Coordinating information security processes

The reflective measures were assessed through internal consistency reliability, indicator reliability, and convergent validity and discriminant validity. Composite reliability and Cronbachs alpha should be higher than 0.7 for adequate internal consistency reliability. Indicator loadings should be higher than 0.7 for acceptable indicator reliability. If the average variance extracted (AVE) yields a value higher than 0.5, convergent validity is established. Discriminant validity is established if the square root of each constructs' AVE is higher than the correlation with any other construct and indicator loadings is higher than all of its crossloadings (Hair et al. 2011). As tables 2 and 3 show, all items were assessed to be both valid and reliable and could thus be used to evaluate the structural model.

	CA	CR	AVE	BBIS	CISP	COS	FKSA	FOS	SFKT
BBIS	0.927	0.949	0.822	**0.907**					
CISP	n/a	n/a	n/a	0.716	n/a				
COS	0.887	0.923	0.750	0.612	0.792	**0.866**			
FKSA	0.749	0.888	0.799	0.624	0.771	0.702	**0.894**		
FOS	1.000	1.000	1.000	0.505	0.684	0.693	0.591	1.000	
SFKT	0.918	0.939	0.754	0.630	0.778	0.824	0.649	0.622	0.868

Table 2: Correlations, Cronbachs alpha, Composite reliability and AVE

	BBIS	**COS**	**FKSA**	**FOS**	**SFKT**
BBIS1	**0.866**	0.575	0.656	0.447	0.537
BBIS2	**0.950**	0.557	0.574	0.483	0.551
BBIS3	**0.939**	0.557	0.523	0.485	0.569
BBIS4	**0.870**	0.529	0.508	0.417	0.620
COS1	0.501	**0.885**	0.630	0.656	0.713
COS2	0.495	**0.910**	0.608	0.649	0.736
COS3	0.503	**0.763**	0.465	0.411	0.690
COS4	0.625	**0.898**	0.712	0.656	0.721
FKSA1	0.657	0.669	**0.901**	0.539	0.604
FKSA2	0.454	0.584	**0.887**	0.516	0.555
FOS1	0.505	0.693	0.591	**1.000**	0.622
SFKT1	0.636	0.698	0.599	0.462	**0.830**
SFKT2	0.392	0.659	0.516	0.605	**0.850**
SFKT3	0.424	0.723	0.509	0.522	**0.864**
SFKT4	0.651	0.744	0.623	0.609	**0.894**
SFKT5	0.616	0.750	0.567	0.501	**0.901**

Table 3: Item loadings and cross loadings for reflective indicators

Finally, the threat of the common methods bias (CMB) was addressed. Ex ante, we addressed CMB by removing two items that we believed our sample were not appropriate to answer (the question was more targeted to end users), counterbalancing the order of questions in the questionnaire to discourage participants from figuring out the relationship between the dependent and independent variables that we were trying to establish. Further, the respondent's anonymity and providing no incentive for completing the survey reduced the likelihood of bias caused by social desirability or respondent acquiescence (P. M. Podsakoff et al. 2003). Ex-post, we performed a test for CMB recommended by Bagozzi et al. (1991) and used by Pavlou et al. (2007) wherein the correlation matrix was examined to identify any highly correlated constructs ($r > 0.9$). In our model, all constructs had correlations below the threshold (Cf. table 2). The ex ante and ex post tests suggest that the possibility of CMB is not of great concern and therefore it's unlikely that CMB confounds the interpretation of the results.

4.2 Evaluation of Structural Model

In order to assess the significance structural path coefficients, bootstrapping re-sampling method with 62 cases and 1000 re-samples was used. The R^2 values of the endogenous constructs measures how much variance is explained by the exogenous constructs. R^2 values of 0.75, 0.50, or 0.25 can be described as substantial, moderate, or weak, respectively. As figure 2 shows, all hypotheses, except H2b are accepted. The R^2 value for the dependent variable of security knowledge sharing is 0.78, which indicates that the constructs in the model explains 78 percent of the variance in the dependent variable. Thus, the proposed model has a strong explanatory power and explains a substantial amount of variance in security knowledge sharing. Organisational structure explains 39 percent of the variance in business-based information security, and together with business-based information security organisational structure explains 78 percent of variance in coordinating information security processes. As security knowledge sharing and organisational structure were operationalised as formative second-order constructs, the significance of the first-order weights were examined. The weights indicated that the each sub-dimension significantly contribute to their underlying factor. Among the determinants of establishment of security knowledge sharing, organisational structure has the strongest direct effect on the dependent variable. The direct effect has a regression coefficient of $\beta = 0.55$. The links between organisational structure and coordinating information security processes and business-based information security are significant, with $\beta = 0.60$ and $\beta = 0.62$, respectively. The link between business-based information security and coordinating information security processes is also significant with $\beta = 0.38$. Finally, coordinating information security have a significant direct effect on knowledge sharing with $\beta = 0.27$. To assess the mediating effect of coordinating information security processes, three tests of mediation was tested using Sobel's (Sobel 1987). The test revealed that coordinating information security processes partly mediates the effect of organisational structure, and fully mediates the effect of business-based information security, on security knowledge sharing. Thus, business-based information security in an organisation affects security knowledge sharing completely trough a processes that coordinates information security. Finally, business-based information security partly mediates the effect of organisational structure on security knowledge sharing.

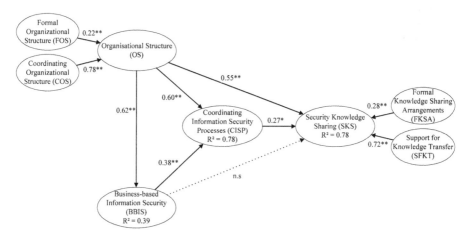

Figure 2: Results of Structural Model Testing

Notes: n.s indicates statistically non-significant; * at $p < 0.05$; and ** at $p < 0.01$.

5. Discussions and Conclusions

This study examines the effect of three organisational factors – organisational structures, business-based information security and coordinating information security processes – in an attempt to increase the understanding of determinants of the establishment of security knowledge sharing in organisations. Based on theoretical understanding, a research model was developed and tested by collecting and analysing data from 62 security executives from a diverse set of organisations located in different geographic regions in the world. The empirical tests of a structural model revealed that all our proposed hypotheses are accepted, except the hypotheses proposing a positive direct link between business-based information security and the establishment of security knowledge sharing. The results of the study imply that organisational structure has a major direct influence on the establishment of security knowledge sharing in organisations. A mediation analysis indicates that the reason for the nonsignificant direct relation is the mediating role of coordinating information security process. The mediation analysis reveals that coordinating information security process has an important role on security knowledge sharing by either partially or fully mediating the effects of organisational structure and business-based information security on security knowledge sharing.

The literature of factors to govern various information security components is often anecdotal or qualitative and has investigated them from a standpoint that assumes their independence from one another. This study therefore provides empirical evidence on what drives organisations' to establish security knowledge sharing.

There exist several limitations which should be taken into account when interpreting the results. First, a general limitation is that we assume that the establishment of security knowledge sharing can be measured using survey methods. Second, although we collected data on type of industry and size of the organisation, we didn't investigate the direct effect of these two factors on the establishment of security knowledge sharing. The reason for this is that we explicitly wanted to investigate governance or management factors that influence security knowledge sharing and not characteristics of the firm. We acknowledge the potential impact of these factors and therefore recommend including them in future work. Third, we collected data from a diverse set of industries and countries and we can therefore say that the study is both a cross-cultural and cross-national study. However, we chose to not highlight this fact, as we believe that the sample size is too small for us to draw any conclusions on identified differences based on this observed heterogeneity which we argue are important to draw if data is collected from multiple industries and countries. It would therefore be interesting to collect more data using our approach to analyse any potential differences based on heterogeneity.

6. References

Anderson, J.C. & Gerbing, D.W., 1991. Predicting the performance of measures in a confirmatory factor analysis with a pretest assessment of their substantive validities. *Journal of Applied Psychology*, 76(5), pp.732–740.

Applegate, S.D., 2009. Social Engineering: Hacking the Wetware! *Information Security Journal: A Global Perspective*, 18(1), pp.40–46.

Armstrong, J.S. & Overton, T.S., 1977. Estimating Nonresponse Bias in Mail Surveys. *Journal of Marketing Research*, 14, pp.396–402.

Bagozzi, R.P., Yi, Y. & Phillips, L.W., 1991. Assessing construct validity in organizational research . *Administrative Science Quarterly*, 36(3), pp.421–458.

Bulgurcu, B., Cavusoglu, H. & Benbasat, I., 2010. Information security policy compliance: an empirical study of rationality-based beliefs and information security awareness. *MIS Quarterly*, 34(3), pp.523–548.

Calder, A. & Watkins, S., 2008. *IT governance A manager's guide to Data Security and ISO 27001/ISO 27002* 4th ed., Kogan Page.

Chang, K. & Wang, C., 2010. Information systems resources and information security. *Information Systems Frontiers*, 13(4), pp.579–593.

Child, J., 1984. *Organization: A guide to Problems and Practice* 2nd ed., London: Paul Chapman Publishing Ltd.

Davenport, T.H. & Prusak, L., 1998. *Working Knowledge: How Organizations Manage What They Know*, Boston : Harvard Business School Press.

Dhillon, G. & Backhouse, J., 2001. Current directions in IS security research: towards socio-organizational perspectives. *Information Systems Journal*, 11(2), pp.127–153.

Dontamsetti, M. & Naranayan, A., 2009. Impact of the Human Element on Information Security. In *Social and Human Elements of Information Security Emerging Trends and Countermeasures*. IGI Global, pp. 27–43.

Drucker, P.F., 1974. New templates for today's organizations. . *Harvard Business Review*, (January-February).

Hair, J.F., Ringle, Christian M. & Sarstedt, M., 2011. PLS-SEM: Indeed a Silver Bullet - Tags: STRUCTURAL equation modeling MARKETING. *Journal of Marketing Theory & Practice*, 19(2), p.139.

Henderson, J.C. & Venkatraman, N., 1993. Strategic alignment: leveraging information technology for transforming organizations. *IBM Systems Journal*, 32(1), pp.4–16.

ISACA, 2006. *Information Security Governance Guidance for Boards of Directors and Executive Management, 2nd Edition,*

Jarvis, C.B., MacKenzie, S.B. & Podsakoff, P.M., 2003. A Critical Review of Construct Indicators and Measurement Model Misspecification in Marketing and Consumer Research. *Journal of Consumer Research*, 30(2), pp.199–218.

Kayworth, T. & Whitten, D., 2010. Effective Information Security Requires a Balance of Social and Technology Factors. *MIS Quartely Executive*, 9(3), pp.303–315.

Kotulic, A.G. & Clark, J.G., 2004. Why there aren't more information security research studies. *Information & Management*, 41(5), pp.597–607.

MacKenzie, S.B., Podsakoff, P.M. & Podsakoff, N.P., 2011. Construct measurement and validation procedures in MIS and behavioral research: integrating new and existing techniques. *MIS Quarterly*, 35(2), pp.293–334.

Paternoster, R. & Simpson, S., 1996. Sanction Threats and Appeals to Morality: Testing a Rational Choice Model of Corporate Crime. *Law & Society Review*, 30(3), pp.549–584.

Pavlou, P.A., Liang, H. & Xue, Y., 2007. Understanding and mitigating uncertainty in online exchange relationships: a principal- agent perspective. *MIS Quarterly*, 31(1), pp.105–136.

Podsakoff, P.M. et al., 2003. Common method biases in behavioral research: a critical review of the literature and recommended remedies. *The Journal of applied psychology*, 88(5), pp.879–903.

Rhodes, J. et al., 2008. Factors influencing organizational knowledge transfer: implication for corporate performance. *Journal of Knowledge Management*, 12(3), pp.84–100.

Ringle, C.M., Wende, S. & Will, A., 2005. SmartPLS.

Rocha Flores, W. & Ekstedt, M., 2012. A Model for Investigation Organizational Impact on Information Security Behavior. In *Seventh Annual Workshop on Information Security and Privacy (WISP) 2012*.

Rocha Flores, W. & Korman, M., 2012. Conceptualization of Constructs for Shaping Information Security Behavior: Towards a Measurement Instrument. In *Seventh Annual Workshop on Information Security and Privacy (WISP) 2012*.

Rogelberg, S.G. & Stanton, J.M., 2007. Introduction: Understanding and Dealing With Organizational Survey Nonresponse. *Organizational Research Methods*, 10(2), pp.195–209.

Segars, A.H. & Grover, V., 1999. Profiles of Strategic Information Systems Planning. *Information Systems Research*, 10(3), pp.199–232.

Siponen, M. & Vance, A., 2010. Neutralization: new insights into the problem of employee systems security policy violations. *MIS Quarterly*, 34(3), pp.487–502.

Sobel, M.E., 1987. Direct and Indirect Effects in Linear Structural Equation Models. *Sociological Methods & Research*, 16(1), pp.155–176.

Sun, L., Ivastave, R.P. & Mock, T.J., 2006. An Information Systems Security Risk Assessment Model Under the Dempster-Shafer Theory of Belief Functions. *Journal of Management Information Systems*, 22(4), pp.109–142.

Appendix

The items that were used are presented as follows:

FOS1: We have an organizational unit with explicit responsibility for organizing and coordinating information security efforts as well as handling incidents.

COS1: There is a committee, comprised of representatives from various business units, which coordinates corporate security initiatives.

COS2: There is a committee, which deals with matters of strategic information security and related decision making.

COS3: Tactical and operative managers are involved in information security decision making, which is related to their unit, responsibilities and/or subordinates.

COS4: In our organization, people responsible for security and representatives from various business units meet to discuss important security issues both formally and informally.

CISP1: Information about risks across business processes is considered.

CISP2: Vulnerabilities in the information systems and related processes are identified regularly.

CISP3: Threats that could harm and adversely affect critical operations are identified regularly (removed)

CISP4: Performance of information security controls is measured, for example with regards to the amount of protection they provide as well as the obtrusiveness and performance limitations they pose to personnel, systems and business activities.

BBIS1: Our security department is very well informed about each unit's business operations, strategies and risks related to them.

BBIS2: Our security department aligns their strategies with our organization's business strategies.

BBIS3: Our security department understands the business goals of our organization.

BBIS4: Strategic decisions on information security policies and solutions are largely business-driven; that is, they are based on business objectives, value, or needs.

FKSA1: Formal information security exercises take place in our organization (e.g., training of backup procedures or reaction on security incidents).

FKSA2: In our organization, there is a formal program for information security awareness, training and education.

SFKT1: Our organization provides informal/voluntary consulting and advisory services in information security for our employees.

SFKT2: There is an intranet site dedicated to information security (e.g., general threats and howtos, policy and guidelines).

SFKT3: There is an intranet site, a quality control system or another information system or portal, which contains work- and task-related information security information such as cues, reminders or warnings bound to an action, process or a situation.

SFKT4: Information technology is actively used to share knowledge and experience regarding information security within our organization.

SFKT5 Our organisation saves and renews important knowledge on both general information security and threats related to information security onto the computer for easy browsing.

Towards a Brain-Compatible Approach for Web-Based, Information Security Education

R Reid and JF Van Niekerk

Institute for ICT Advancement, Port Elizabeth, South Africa
e-mail: S208045820@live.nmmu.ac.za; Johan.vanniekerk@nmmu.ac.za

Abstract

Information Security is becoming a necessity for all information users. Suitable delivery and presentation of information security education to these users is therefore becoming increasingly important. Online learning may be a suitable mechanism. It has become a widely used, extensive education format that uses information and communication technology as well as the many resources available on the web. In order to ensure an effective and enjoyable learning experience online education should emulate real-world 'classroom education' and be designed in compliance with pedagogy. Brain-compatible education (BCE) is such a pedagogy. BCE has primarily been used in real-world classrooms. This paper examines how generic, online, information security education can be developed in compliance with BCE principles in the Moodle environment.

Keywords

Information Security Education, Brain-compatible Education, E-learning, Moodle, Case study

1. Introduction

Information security education had long been an acknowledged need in an organisational context (NIST 800-16 1998). However due to recent changes in and the creation of new national legislation and cyber security initiatives, this need has now been assigned to the organisation and the general public. The educational target audience therefore includes individuals from all age groups, education levels and social standings. The current generation would be the most affected by this change.

The current generation of learners has grown up in a media-rich environment. This environment has predisposed them to prefer information presented in an entertaining and interactive manner. Consequently, this generation will be the first capable of benefiting from the educational aspects of the web and interactive web technologies.

Educational approaches which use computer network technologies, primarily over an intranet or the Internet, to deliver information and instruction to individuals are fast becoming a popular education method (Welsh et al. 2003). It has many advantages such as easy accessibility, target audience diversity and development versatility. Unfortunately web-based learning courses often mirror real classrooms. Therefore in many educational fields including information security, the problems that exist in real classrooms also exist in web-based learning environments.

Educational researchers are continuously searching for pedagogies that can improve the learning experience in any real classroom. Many of these pedagogies could potentially also be applied in online environments. Brain-compatible education (BCE) is one such pedagogy that has been successfully used in real classrooms.

Brain-compatible education is designed to take advantage of the relationship between an educational environment and the natural complexities of the human brain (Jensen 2008). Several BCE principles, methods and techniques have thus developed. These techniques endeavour to teach subject matter in a manner and format which is naturally complimentary to the brain's physical and psychological processing functions (R. N. Caine & G. Caine 1991). BCE's application to the design of online learning environments has been proposed by Clemons (2005), this paper will apply and test it on an online information security course.

This paper aims to show that BCE principles *can* be applied in the Moodle 2.0 environment when developing an information security course to be appealing and effective for a learner's information security education experience. The methodology which was used is presented in the next section.

2. Methodology

This paper takes the form and structure of a case study, as described by Creswell (2007). The structure is as follows: an entry vignette, introduction, description of the case and its context, development of issues, detail about the selected issues, assertions, and closing vignette.

The research itself was conducted as a case study wherein material from an existing information security course was selected and modified to comply with BCE principles in the Moodle environment. Some of the changes made where previously theorised possible by Reid, Van Niekerk and Von Solms (2011). This paper focuses on the lessons learned during the actual implementation of the design guidelines which could be applicable in future online, BCE cyber security courses.

3. Context of Case study

SEAT was the course selected for modification during the case study. SEAT is a security education and training course at the Nelson Mandela Metropolitan University (NMMU) which targets students and the general public. Its objectives are: to improve awareness of the need to protect system resources and an organizations end users; to develop the skills and knowledge of computer users so they may securely perform their computer activities; to allow online access to a rich source of security related best practices; to help end users understand why security is part of their responsibilities, and how they impact their organizational employers security.

The original SEAT consisted of nine modules. Each module consisted of a single flash lesson and a related multiple choice quiz. The lessons content presentation consisted of text and related clipart images. An evaluation of the original SEAT showed that it lacked usability, which necessitated the redevelopment of the course.

Two major additional considerations during redevelopment included the need for it to be as appealing and easily accessible as possible for a diverse, dispersed target audience. Thus it was decided that the course would be modified to be presented in a BCE compliant manner, and made accessible as an e-learning course via Moodle.

4. Case study Background

This section will provide a brief background to the primary fields of study which influenced the choices in the redesign of SEAT as presented later in this paper.

4.1. Online Learning

Many communications, collaboration and education enabling technologies have developed alongside the Internet, computer-based multimedia, and the World Wide Web. These technologies have become an enabler of a new variety of e-learning called "web-based" or "online" learning (Zhang 2003).

Online education has delivered many benefits to education experiences including: improved quality of the learning, improved accessibility to education and training, improved cost-effectiveness of education (Alexander 2001), promotion lifelong learning, enhancement of an educators ability to address different audiences and diversify their teaching style, and use of innovative teaching methods in order to maintain students' interest (Bates 2001).

Educators have focused on extending traditional learning method and techniques through electronic and web technologies into new dynamic education models and environments (Eckert et al. 1997). Many web-based learning environments complete with material have already been successfully created using a variety of tools. Selecting such a tool was the first consideration.

Many popular, open-source and proprietary learning system tools such as Blackboard, Sakai, aTutor, Schoology and many others exist. Moodle is one such environment which is used at Nelson Mandela Metropolitan University (NMMU). Therefore, due to convenience and availability of this platform, it was chosen for the case study. However the similarities which exist between the various online learning management systems and their supporting web-technologies, may mean that this case studies assertions may be applicable to other platforms. The next consideration was engaging the learners.

The aim of any educational experience is to ensure learners accept, retain, and process information which is presented to them during a learning experience. To fulfil this goal the learners should be interested, engaged and motivated to participate in the learning experience. Learning principles and conditions should therefore be used to present material in a manner which meets learner needs (Clemons 2005). The application of pedagogy to e-learning courses is therefore recommended.

4.2. Brain-compatible Education

Brain-compatible education (BCE) is defined as learning based on principles, methods and techniques which endeavour to teach content in a manner and format which is naturally complimentary to the brains physical and psychological processing function for incorporating information into its schema (Jensen 2005).

Brain-based education involves teaching through the designing and orchestrating life-like, enriching, and appropriate experiences for learners (R. N. Caine & G. Caine 1991). It is a pedagogy which addresses multiple modes of learning, acknowledge outlets for creative presentation of learning, provide enough contrast to preclude boredom, and contribute to a motivating context (Rogers & Renard 1999). It accomplishes this by using effective teaching methods, techniques and approaches from all educational disciplines to enhance subject matter to be as appealing and learnable as possible for the brains of the target students (Jensen 2008).

Target audiences for classroom-based BCE learners have ranged from primary school to university students. The application of this pedagogy has been proven to positively affect students' learning (Jensen 2005). Clemons (2005) suggested the application of the pedagogy to online, but did not provide any technical details on how this could be done. This paper aims to explain **how** the pedagogy can be implemented in a Moodle context for an information security course.

4.3. Moodle

"Moodle is an Open Source Course Management System (CMS), also known as a Learning Management System (LMS) or a Virtual Learning Environment (VLE)" developed in compliance with a "social constructionist pedagogy" (Moodle.org 2012). It is a tool used by educators to create dynamic, online websites for the delivery of their course to their students.

Moodle courses consist of an educator's chosen activities and resources. An activity is something that a student will do that interacts with other students and or the teacher (Moodle.org 2012). There are thirteen standard Moodle some examples being assignments, forums, wikis, quizzes and lessons (Moodle.org 2012). A resource is an item that an educator can use to support learning (Moodle.org 2012). Standard resources included by Moodle are files, folders, IMS content packages, labels, HTML pages and URLs. All courses can be augmented through the use of plug-ins.

Moodle can be used to conduct entirely online courses or it can be used as an augmentation tool for their interpersonal classes (Moodle.org 2012). NNMU has mainly used it as an augmenter tool; however with the creation of SEAT it is also being used as the sole material provider for an entirely online effort.

For the purposes of the case study presented in this paper, Moodle was the chosen LMS for the implementation of a BCE compatible version of SEAT. The next section will identify the issues which were addressed in the case study.

5. Identification of Issues

This section will briefly outline a few issues addressed by the redevelopment of the SEAT course. The problems are separated into two categories: Learner-related and Educational-Material Related.

5.1. Learner-Material Issues

Many issues/factors required addressing so as to improve the learners education experience. The first issue is that the target audience is the general public. Therefore the material has to cater for a large variety of learning style preferences. Furthermore because the audience is so varied in age, abilities, background and culture etc. the material had to be as appealing as possible to as many people as possible.

The second issue is that in traditional, 'compulsory learning' schools or organisations are able to "force" the completion of an activity or course through cohesion of various forms; in a *voluntary* online education scenario this cannot be replicated. Therefore alternative measures must be used to motivate a learner to learn. Thirdly the existing SEAT material encouraged learning by rote. This an issue because remembering material by rote is the lowest level of Blooms taxonomy of the cognitive domains (Van Niekerk 2010). Cyber Security Education learners need to understand the material so as to be able to apply it.

The fourth issue is that the current standard material is presented in a non-explanatory manner. As a result of this presentation style, the learners are often distracted by other activities. The fifth issue is that the modules are currently presented as isolated segments of the course with no tie into the overall concept of what is being taught. The context in which the material is taught is also not always relevant for a student. Finally in the original material no feedback was provided to the learners. This is problematic, as formative feedback is necessary in any education approach. This concludes the learner –material issues, the next section will identify the material-creation issues.

5.2. Material-Creation Issues

In addition to the learner related factors; discussed above; factors such as how the material is developed, hosted and accessed also needed to be addressed. Firstly the original application was difficult to maintain. This is because code maintenance, over a number of years, was poorly documented. This is further aggravated by the fact that the development language and development environment used to create the original SEAT is outdated and no longer functions well on current computers. Thirdly the material was not very accessible. Learners required access to an installation of a desktop application, this limited a learner's ability to access the material to traditional class and lab time. Finally there was no automated control over who could enrol in the course and therefore the course "graduate" was tracked manually. Therefore this system was vulnerable to human error.

The issues identified in each category will each be elaborated upon in the next section. The solutions applied in the redevelopment of the material will be provided.

6. Detail of selected Issues

This section elaborates upon the previously discussed issues which will be further explained and related to the brain-compatible pedagogical principles. For additional brain-compatible principle explanations refer to Reid et al. (2011). The brain-compatible principles which will be addressed are listed in Table 1. Each principle has been assigned a non-meaningful number which, for the sake of convenience, will be used for all further references to the same principle within the paper.

	Principle
1	A learning experience should be as multifaceted as possible; catering for many learning styles and providing as many opportunities for each learner to develop as possible.
2	Positive emotions should be used to aid recognition and recall.
3	It is necessary to repetitively review material to solidify recall and recognition.
4	Both focused and peripheral attention of a learner should be involved in the learning process.
5	Every brain simultaneously perceives and creates parts and wholes during the learning process.
6	Relate all new material back to old material and thereby build new knowledge on old knowledge
7	Allow learners to progress through the course at their own pace.

Table 2: Brain-compatible education principles

The original material of the SEAT course was moved to the Moodle environment. Once it had migrated the authors began the process of updating the material and course to solve the various issues. The redevelopment of the course will now be explained.

6.1. Learner-Material Issues

Firstly it was determined that to implement Principle 5 learners had to understand how material exiting as an isolated concept and as a part of an overall cyber security approach. To do this Moodle's ability to separate course material into modules and blocks was used. Each lesson from the seat course was assigned to a module. Within each module a lesson activity, a quiz and additional resources were included.

Modules were structured in a progressive sequence. Initially only the first module was accessible. To progress through the course the learners had to achieve a minimum required mark in each modules quiz. This progressive design was it ensured the material was viewed in a particular order. This aided principles 5 and 6. The content could relate material back to the previous modules material, ensured that learners had the required "old" knowledge and provided perspective as to how the concept fitted into the whole subject.

Within the module itself the learners were free to navigate through the lesson material and the additional resources according to their own preferences. The grouping of the activities and resources complied with Clemons' (2005) suggestion of "chunking" activities together to help them relate and make sense. By allowing learners to review the modules material in any particular order they were allowed to progress as a self-determined pace. This combined with the allowance for the active modules quiz to be completed at any time promotes Principle 7.

Schools or organisations can insure the completion of traditional compulsory learning activities through cohesion of various forms. In a voluntary online education scenario this cannot be replicated. Therefore alternative measures must be used to motivate a learner to learn. Learning requires motivation and engagement this is particularly important since online learning is a self-managed endeavour.

The next aspect of the redevelopment dealt with the redevelopment of the material itself. This redevelopment had to aid compliance with the Brain-compatible principles 1, 2, 3, 4 and 6.

Initially, the Moodle lesson activity was considered for the SEAT lessons. Moodle lessons allow navigation between question pages and content pages, and it has adaptive ability to navigate between pages based on the learner's response. However because the lessons consist of basic HTML it was determined that they were not dynamic enough for our needs. Instead, Microsoft's Sketchflow Silverlight application was used to create lessons which were then hosted on a server as a webpage. This webpage was then embedded in the Moodle module as a URL resource. The aim was to create interactive, media-rich and engaging lesson material.

The Moodle course targets the general public. This means that the learner audience consisted of individuals who varied their age group, culture, experiences, abilities and learning-style preferences. The course material had to appeal to as many of these individuals as possible to ensure successful learning experience. To enable the brain-compatible principles 1 and 2 were applied to the redevelopment of the material.

Clemons (2005) suggested the inclusion of "elaborate rehearsal" and interactivity in an online course to aid compliance with these principles. Activities which Clemons theorised complied with her suggestions were audio-,video- and animation clips, role plays, debates, voice-overs lectures, use of colour, diagrams, charts, pictures, interactive models and drawing activities.

In the redeveloped SEAT we included video clips, music, and lesson materials containing text, contextual pictures and clarifying animations. Colour was used to influence the learner's emotional state.

The background of the lesson material was styled yellow; this elicits positive moods and aimed to attract the learner's attention. This aspect of the material also related to Principle 4 and the enhancement of the; learners attentive ness. Future modifications of the material will incorporate green into the colour scheme as it encourages productivity and long-term energy are good in classrooms (Taylor 2007). Because of

NMMU policy, the Moodle environment itself was styled to conform to the NMMU, colour branding which is not necessarily brain-compatible. This will be tested in future research.

Clemons (2005) suggested that interaction would enhance attentiveness in online courses. The use of techniques to stimulate emotions such as excitement, fun, curiosity and anticipation to enhance learning (Clemons 2005). All this aids compliance with principles 1,2,3 and 5. Role-playing and scenario simulations and thought provoking games, videos and animations were suggested by Clemons as suitable techniques. Unfortunately role-playing and scenario simulations are currently only planned features of Moodle (Moodle.org 2012). To resolve this issue we included video resources and animations which illustrated the concepts in an interactive manner in the material. These additions also aimed to focus the learner's attention on the material and prevent distractions (principle 4).

Principle 3 was reinforced multiple time since the material was provided in many formats and included many elements which repeated the concepts in different contexts while appealing to principle 1 by catering for all learning styles.

Finally the courses and its quizzes and exams were modified to provide formative feedback. This modification complied with Clemons (2005) suggestion of providing encouraging, positive feedback and avoid penalizing mistakes that come from the learning curve associated with technology.

6.2. Material-Creation Issues

There are many ways the brain-compatible principles can be applied in the Moodle environment. The applications used in this case study to aid the learners in their interaction with course material are only a few examples of this. The next section will address how the issues relating to the materials creation and hosting were dealt with.

The Technology Acceptance Model (TAM) indicates that when users are presented with a new technology the perceived usefulness and ease-of-use will influence their decision about how and when they will use it (Venkatesh & Davis 2000).

Since the online material was designed for Moodle, the material had to be hosted on a Moodle server. NMMU has an internal campus-wide Moodle server. The use of Moodle addressed most of the issues in this category.

The issue of accessibility was partially solved because Moodle can be accessed online. Learners are able to access their Learn sites anywhere at any time. However currently the NMMU Moodle server only allows registered NMMU students to log in and register for courses. Internal policies have issued a practice of disabling manual registration procedures. Therefore a lecturer cannot register a student who is not physically studying at NMMU. This issue will be addressed by moving the SEAT course to an external server.

The material is now maintainable as the Moodle platform is constantly be updated by its developers and all the changes are well documented. The actual lesson material used in the SEAT case study is also updateable and editable via Microsoft tools e.g. Expression blend and Visual Studio 2010. All Microsoft projects are backwards compatible.

Moodle's multitude of features are very useful in the creation and design of an education experience. However the default, online creation methods of various activities are not always ideal, and can be tedious or time consuming e.g. the quiz development feature. The native Moodle quiz interface was time consuming and not ideal for the development of many questions simultaneously. We used a third-party tool called Respondus as an alternative.

7. Assertions/Lesson Learned

Firstly based on a preliminary evaluation of the learner's reactions to the redeveloped material we have found the following: 100% of the learners liked the look and feel of the material; 85% of the learners like the variety of educational material provided; and 80% of the learners felt motivated and engaged during the learning experience.

Secondly the authors wish to assert that based on the case study's course redevelopment and subsequent launch that it **is** possible to create brain-compatible, online information security material. Furthermore it has been well demonstrated that Moodle enables the development of brain-compatible information material even though it is created to enable a different pedagogy. It should however be noted that the creation process is not always easy, and the built-in development tools are not always very usable or suitable for mass development. The authors recommend the employment of third-party tools when necessary.

Finally, it is the opinion of the authors that there is a requirement for the development of tools which cater specifically for information security educators who wish to create brain-compatible education material.

8. Conclusion

Moodle is an education platform which can be used in compliance with BCE principles to create online, information security. However some of its creation features are not as comprehensive or usable as they could be. In these cases the use of third-party party tools is recommended. To further enable information security educators to create online, brain-compatible, information security education material, both using and independent of Moodle, a layer of applications and tools which cater specifically for the needs of material creating educators needs to be developed.

9. References

Alexander, S., 2001. E-learning developments and experiences. *Education + Training*, 42(4/5), pp.240-248.

Bates, T., 2001. *National strategies for e-learning in post-secondary education and training*, Available at: www.unesco.org/iiep.

Caine, R.N. & Caine, G., 1991. *Making Connections: Teaching and the Human Brain.*, Alexandria, VA: Association for Supervision and Curriculum Development.

Clemons, S.A., 2005. Brain-Based Learning: Possible Implications for Online Instruction. *International Journal of Instructional Technology & Distance Learning*, 2(9).

Creswell, J.W., 2007. *Qualitative inquiry and research design*, Sage Publications, Inc.

Eckert, A., Geyer, W. & Effelsberg, W., 1997. A distance learning system for higher education based on tele-communications and multimedia: A compund organizationsl, pedagogical and technical approach. In *ED-Media/Ed-Telecom*. Calgary, Canada.

Jensen, E.P., 2008.A fresh look at brain-based education. *PhiDeltaKappan*, 89(6), pp.408-417.

Jensen, E.P., 2005. *Teaching with the brain in mind* 2nd ed., Alexandria, VA: Association for Supervision and Curriculum Development.

Moodle.org, 2012. About Moodle. *Moodle.org*. Available at: http://moodle.org/about/ [Accessed June 19, 2012].

NIST 800-16, 1998. NIST 800-16. *National Institute of Standards and Technology - Nist Special Publication*.

Van Niekerk, J., 2010. *Fostering Information Security Culture Through Integrating Theory and Technology*. Nelson Mandela Metropolitan University.

Reid, R., Van Niekerk, J. & Von Solms, R., 2011. Guidelines for the creation of brain-compatible cyber security educational material in Moodle 2 . 0. In *Information Security South Africa (ISSA)*. Johannesburg, pp. 1-8.

Rogers, S. & Renard, L., 1999. Relationship Driven Teaching. *Educational Leadership*, 57(1), pp.34-37.

Taylor, A., 2007. How the Brain Learns Best. *Journal of Adventist Education*, pp.42-45.

Venkatesh, V. & Davis, F.D., 2000. A Theoretical Extension of the Technology Acceptance Model: Four Longitudinal Field Studies. *Management Science*, 46(2), pp.186-204.

Welsh, E.T. et al., 2003. E-learning : emerging uses , empirical results and future directions. *International Journal of Training and Development*, 7(4), pp.245-258.

Zhang, D., 2003. Powering E-Learning In the New Millennium : An Overview of E-Learning and Enabling Technology. *Information Systems Frontiers*, 5(2), pp.201-212.

Using Theories and Best Practices to Bridge the Phishing Gap

E.D Frauenstein and R. von Solms

Nelson Mandela Metropolitan University, School of ICT, Port Elizabeth, South Africa
e-mail: efrauenstein@wsu.ac.za[1] and rossouw@nmmu.ac.za[2]

Abstract

Phishing is a mounting security problem that organisations and users continue to face. Organisations generally apply a single-layer level of defence against information security threats, which includes phishing. This single-layer level of defence is certainly not adequate against modern-day phishing attacks. It is essential for organisations to implement a holistic approach, while considering human factors, organisational aspects and technological controls to combat phishing threats. However, in each of these three elements, weaknesses arise as each is linked by means of human involvement. As a result, this approach creates a gap for successful phishing attacks to potentially compromise these elements. This paper suggests possible linkages to cover the 'gaps' between each of these elements. More understanding is necessary on how these linkages can be managed more appropriately. As such, this paper introduces possible theories and best practices which can be used to understand and address each of these linkages and therefore attempts to bridge the phishing gap by strengthening the human element.

Keywords

Phishing, social engineering, human factors, information security, agency theory, Technology Acceptance Model. COBIT 4.1

1. Introduction

We live in the information age where users are able to access and share information freely by using both computers and mobile devices. Although this has been made possible by the Internet, it poses security risks as attempts are made to use this same Internet environment in order to compromise information. Accordingly, there is an urgent need for users and organisations to protect their information resources from agents presenting a security threat. Apart from dedicating resources, organisations typically spend large amounts of money as well to improve their technological defences against general security threats. However, the agents posing these threats are adopting social engineering (SE) techniques in order to bypass the technical measures which organisations are putting in place. SE techniques are often effective because they target human behaviour; something which the majority of researchers believe is a far easier alternative than hacking information systems. Typically, phishing involves a fraudster (referred to as a phisher) who uses SE techniques in the context of an email message in order to steal confidential information from a user by imitating a legitimate entity (Kumaraguru *et al.* 2007). Most of the organisations cited in such phishing emails are well-known financial institutions. Using email is the most effective phishing device because the email message may be created to appear authentic through the use of the corporate logos and terminology distinctive of the institution from which the email is purported to originate. Typically, phishers use a fabricated story to convince their victims either to resolve a particular problem or to claim a substantial prize. The user is usually also required to complete this process by clicking on a hyperlink contained within the email. This hyperlink then typically directs the user to a spoofed website which requires the victim to log in using personal information (e.g. username, password, account number). The user believes that the spoofed website is genuine because it looks almost identical to the legitimate website. However, the user is unaware of the fact that the spoofed website records his/her personal information which will then be used towards the phisher's own ends.

A cyber security study conducted by Deloitte revealed that chief information security officers (CISOs) are of the opinion that phishing and pharming currently pose the highest cyber security threat to their organisations (Deloitte, 2012). Organisations and their customers have lost millions of dollars as a result of phishing. In view of the fact that there are no boundaries to the Internet, phishing may affect all users who are connected to the Internet. The power of phishing lies in its ability to circumvent technological defences because it exploits human behaviour and knowledge. Dhamija *et al.* (2006) believe that users generally have great difficulty in distinguishing between legitimate websites and spoofed websites. However, despite this, organisations continue to focus primarily on securing their computer systems using technological controls and, thus, neglecting the human element. Within an organisational context, Frauenstein and Von Solms (2009) pointed out that there are a number of areas which phishers attack and attempt to exploit. These areas or elements include; human factors, organisational aspects and technological controls (HOT). Ironically, these same areas serve simultaneously as security measures against phishing attacks. In the literature studied, the main areas of HOT are often treated as separate or disjoint entities. Furthermore, these three elements mentioned above are characterised by gaps which arise resulting from human involvement (Frauenstein and Von Solms, 2011). Phishers target these gaps. This paper proposes possible 'linkages' between these elements. By strengthening the human element in each of these elements and the gap between them, an integrated approach can be formed which will ultimately result in a holistic anti-phishing framework.

2. Using an Integrated HOT Approach to Address Phishing

Beznosov and Beznosova (2007) state "public research related to computer security has been overwhelmingly focused on technological aspects, leaving human and social elements mostly uncharted". The literature also recognises that technology is not the only way to manage general information security related threats. Subsequently, human factors became another important focus for information security research. Furthermore, to understand why users behave and react in certain ways when presented with difficult situations, human psychology (Jakobsson, 2007; Schneier, 2008; West, 2008), human-computer interaction, user security awareness (Thomson and Von Solms, 1998), attitudes and behaviour (Downs *et al.* 2007), and organisational culture (Cabrera *et al.* 2001; Schlienger and Teufel, 2003; Thomson *et al.* 2006) are all distinct areas of interest in the area of human factors. Cabrera *et al.* (2001) emphasise that technology and people are only two of the several subsystems that function within the organisation. They suggest that in order to understand the interconnections between technology and people, a broader scope which describes the relationships between the two and other important subsystems needs to be employed. Besides technology, Werlinger *et al.* (2008) see a need to understand the impact of human and organisational factors. They state that few researchers have provided a comprehensive integrated overview of the challenges faced by security practitioners. Furthermore, they add that "a better understanding of how different human, organisational and technological elements interplay could explain how different factors lead to security breaches and vulnerabilities within an organisation". Besnosov and Beznosova (2007) recommend that future research should focus on examining the *relationship* between organisational processes and behaviour in the effectiveness of security defences. In their research, Cabrera *et al.* (2001) reveal that an integrative model will help both administrators and technology designers to understand and manage the interconnections between technology and the other human and organisational aspects of their business. Furthermore, they state that it is important to pay special attention to the factors that determine the behaviour of people in a particular organisation. Moreover, they maintain that organisational culture needs to be understood as it will describe factors that influence human behaviour. This would seem to support the need to explore the factors that influence these relationships.

In this paper, the 'integrated approach' consists of merging three main elements, namely, human factors, organisational aspects and technological controls (HOT). Since each element has its own inherent weaknesses, even when an element is linked to another element (e.g. H+T), the gap for phishers to exploit is not eliminated. As pointed out by Werlinger *et al.* (2008), these gaps become more apparent if elements are interrelated because of these relationships. Some sources discuss adopting an approach whereby all HOT elements are included and, therefore, some studies have already partly integrated some of the elements. However, it would also seem from the literature studied that there are challenges using this approach. An understanding of how to integrate these elements is necessary, as failure to achieve this could result in one relationship being compromised and thus may have an undesired effect on other elements.

3. A Need to Bridge the Phishing Gap

This section aims to further explore the links between HOT elements by using problem-based scenarios. At the same time, this section also points out the gaps between each of these relationships. Understanding which relationships depend on one another will help establish which of the main HOT relationships require strengthening.

> Scenario A: John receives an email from his banking institution. The email warns John that the bank's customers may be subject to fraudulent activities. Therefore, he is requested to verify his banking details to validate his account. The email provides a hyperlink which will direct him to the bank's website in order to complete this verification process.

In this scenario, John will have to know how to discern phishing emails from legitimate emails. Accordingly, this knowledge will determine his actions and behaviour in reaction to the email. In this scenario, the technological controls had failed, as the phishing email reached John, consequently exposing the human factor element, and thus making John vulnerable. Alternatively, if John had not received the phishing email, then the technological controls might have performed their role adequately. In this scenario, John could make effective use of technological tools such as an anti-virus program and/or features of the email client. If he could correctly identify the phishing email, then he could use the email client function to mark the email as spam, possibly preventing such emails from reaching him again in the future. John could also identify warnings from his web browser whether he is active on a spoofed-website. In these instances, only a single-layer defence is present, that is, either technological controls or human factors. Therefore, it can be established that in Scenario A, **human** (H) and **technological** (T) elements are linked (HT) and require further strengthening.

> Scenario B: John manages to find time during working hours to communicate with his friends on his office computer terminal using social networking websites and other applications. From his computer terminal, he also manages to download software, games, movies, wallpapers and music, as he does not have an Internet connection at home.

Phishers make use of a variety of technologies and techniques to trick their victims and John may not be aware that phishing is not limited to the use of emails. In Scenario B, it would seem that John disregards any security risks he might pose to the organisation from his actions. Through social networking websites, John may have clicked on hyperlinks, supposedly sent from his online friends, thereby downloading a virus or having his account hijacked. John is abusing organisational resources by using its Internet service for his personal interests. He is also abusing organisational time, as he is not carrying out his work-related tasks. John is being paid to perform his duties at work and not for any personal activities. Activities, such as downloading games, could potentially expose the organisation to viruses or Trojans, which may originate from phishers. A control mechanism related to Scenario B, could be organisational policies and procedures that strictly manage the use of technology by employees; for example, an Internet usage policy. Weak policies could result in employees bringing in their own technology from home, further creating new opportunities for phishers and other threats. Policies and procedures can also help ensure that John understands what encompasses acceptable and unacceptable behaviour in the workplace. John should be aware of the risks that security threats pose to him personally, as well as be technically knowledgeable about using websites, hyperlinks, email clients, software and so on. In Scenario B, it is evident that there is a clear gap between John's needs and what the organisation expects and requires from John. In this instance, the main links that can be compromised by John's actions are the **human** (H) and **organisational** (O) elements.

Scenario C: The organisation has very slow Internet connection and sometimes no Internet at all. As a result, staff often blames the organisation for not completing tasks on time. Moreover, the computer hardware and software are outdated and the organisation has no clearly defined policies or procedures describing the acceptable use of software or placing any restrictions on its use. In addition, individuals do not require authorisation to enter the work premises. Although staff security training workshops are offered, staff members do not participate and generally exempt themselves from such training.

In Scenario C, it is evident, that, from a technological perspective, the organisation is not providing a suitable service. It should ensure that technical staff apply technological controls such as network firewalls and anti-virus programs, and ensure that they are updated regularly and managed correctly. The organisation could restrict users (employees) from accessing social networking websites from their workstations during work time or even permanently by implementing technological controls such as firewalls and other authentication measures. The organisation is not implementing good practice in that it does not use technology to carry out business functions correctly, accurately and efficiently. As a result, opportunities may be created for phishers to expose any weaknesses inherent in the systems. Outdated hardware and software, viruses (perhaps originating from phishers) are able to penetrate the organisation's weakened information system and compromise its information and data. Moreover, since this organisation has no access control measures in place, any unauthorised person may enter the premises posing as an employee or customer. This imposter could be a social engineer (i.e. phisher) intent on analysing any physical, technical and behavioural weaknesses in the system. Consequently this information could be used to plot a phishing attack on the organisation. From this scenario it is evident that there is a gap between the **organisational** (O) and **technological** (T) elements.

In all three scenarios the human element was targeted most frequently, even though other controls played a role. Unfortunately, organisations may therefore be of the opinion that, since phishing penetrates technological defences, technology requires the most improvement. However, phishers most frequently exploit human behaviour which is made easier by a lack of knowledge in correct use of technology. Furthermore, humans' lack of compliance with organisational policies and procedures favours phishers. In order, therefore, to be adequately protected against phishing attacks, particularly in an organisational context, a framework is required consisting of all the HOT elements (Frauenstein and Von Solms, 2009). There is a need to close the gap between each of these elements. If this is not done, any of the three HOT elements may subsequently be compromised to the detriment of the organisation. In the literature examined no approach could be found that describes ways to further integrate and improve the relationships between the HOT elements.

4. Linking Elements towards a Holistic Framework

The previous section established and described the three main links that should exist between the HOT elements. However, these links are still not tightly bound, thus exposing a gap for phishers to exploit. As such, more understanding is necessary on how the links can be managed more appropriately. This section aims to achieve this by describing theories and best practices in conjunction with those links. An understanding of these theories and best practices will help point out specific areas that influence the respective links, which will contribute to the establishment of an anti-phishing framework.

4.1. The Technology Acceptance Model

Many IT professionals reason that the key to the success of information security lies in the way humans use computers and technology. Phishers take advantage of aspects of human behaviour, specifically the way humans interact with computers (Schneier, 2000). Since it is apparent that humans are often unable to use technology optimally, developers are generally automating technology. One of the factors that may cause humans not to use technology correctly is because it is considered technically complex. The Technology Acceptance Model (TAM) is an information systems theory representing individuals' acceptance and usage of technology (Davis, 1989). For this reason, the TAM serves as a suitable model to understand how the **human** (H) and **technology** (T) elements can be further strengthened. According to Swanson (1988), one of the most challenging issues in information systems (IS) research is to understand why people accept or reject computers. If this can be understood, one would be able to predict, explain and increase user acceptance of technology (Davis, 1989). Accordingly, the TAM suggests that when users are presented with a new form of technology, a number of factors influence their decision about *how* and *when* they will use that technology. As discussed by Davis (1989), these two factors are: perceived ease of use (PEOU) and perceived usefulness (PU). Users' negative attitudes and behaviour towards the use of technology may influence its perceived usefulness.

In his study Ohaya (2006) points out the following factors why users are still susceptible to phishing: "lack of knowledge in computer systems; lack of security and security indicators; lack of attention to security indicators; lack of attention to the absence of security indicators and finally sophistication of spoofed websites." In some cases, users ignore phishing warning messages from anti-phishing tools (Dhamija *et al.* 2006; Egelman *et al.* 2008). All of these concerns mentioned points out a lack of knowledge in technology. Technology is frequently used by phishers as a tool to carry out their attacks. In response, users (the victims) should also be able to use technology as a tool to protect themselves against such attacks. Some phishers are very knowledgeable about web development and are able to develop websites that are almost perfect replicas of genuine websites (Jakobsson, 2007). This strongly suggests that users need to be educated, trained and made aware of phishing techniques and to be suspicious of well-designed spoofed websites. Users also require training in using technological tools and its features such as email client, web browser, anti-virus program, system alerts and so on. This can successfully bridge the gap between humans (H) and technology (T).

4.2. Agency Theory

Agency theory discusses the agency problem that arises when cooperating parties have different goals and division of labour (Jensen and Meckling, 1976). This relationship is metaphorically described as a contract between two parties, namely, the *principal* who delegates work to the *agent* who performs that work (Jensen and Meckling, 1976). In this study, the research problem is addressed in an organisational context; as such, the principal is seen as the *organisation* and the agent is the *user* or *employee*. Agency theory is regarded here as being an appropriate theory to understand the significant role between **human** (employee) and **organisational** (management) elements. According to Eisenhardt (1989), agency theory is concerned with resolving two problems: The conflicting desires or goals of the principal and agent, and the verification of the agent's activities, which is too difficult or expensive for the principal. Conflict arises when the principal and the agent have different attitudes toward risk. These differing goals may explain why the agent (i.e. employees) disobeys or neglects organisational policies and procedures. The fact that organisations have policies and procedures in place means that there are no written disparities in what the employee should and should not do. However, even if an organisation has such policies and procedures in place, it should not necessarily be taken for granted that employees comply with and support them. Herath and Rao (2009) state that employee negligence and non-compliance with policies cost organisations millions of dollars every year. To address the problems pointed out above, the principal aims to motivate the agent using incentives that recognise the agent's effort, as well as the environmental factors that have an effect on the outcomes (Herath and Rao, 2009).

Schlienger and Teufel (2003) describe that even where employees know of security policies, they may still wilfully ignore such policies because they do not understand *why* they are needed. Therefore, for users to behave appropriately in the organisation they first need to be made aware of and given reasons why security policies and procedures are needed. Furthermore, they need to know and understand how to implement the procedures supporting such policies (Thomson and Von Solms, 1998). If this is not accomplished, users will put organisations' information at risk. Educating employees on why such policies are in place not only increases understanding, but also increases motivation (Siponen, 2000). In terms of such policies, it is also important that employees understand their roles and responsibilities within the organisation (ISO/IEC 27002, 2005, p. 23). Establishing an organisational security culture is another element that cannot be ignored as it has great significance in agency theory. The organisational culture is consequently expressed in terms of the collective values, norms and knowledge of organisations (Schlienger and Teufel, 2003). In turn, those collective norms and values impact on the behaviour of the organisation's employees. If employees do not take the severity of risks posed by phishers seriously, their behaviour will affect other members of a particular organisation. Addressing the agency theory factors requires both parties to understand their roles and responsibilities. In this regard, education is required to help change the behaviour of employees. If this could be achieved, this would satisfy the agency theory problems highlighted earlier, thus closing the gap between the human (H) and the organisational (O) elements.

4.3.   COBIT 4.1

Linking IT to business is not a new concept; it has previously been recognised as business–IT alignment. This alignment refers to "applying IT in an appropriate and timely way, in harmony with the business strategies, goals and needs" (Luftman, 2004). IT alignment specifically attempts to address the way the organisation should or could be harmonised with IT. For this reason, COBIT 4.1 (2007) serves as a suitable best practice to understand how the link between the **organisational** (O) and **technology** (T) elements can be strengthened. COBIT's objective is the following: "Specifying the decision rights and accountability framework to encourage desirable behaviour in the use of IT." It has been frequently pointed out in this study, that human behaviour is a concern. IT governance implies a system in which all stakeholders, including the board, executive management, customers and staff, have clear accountability for their respective responsibilities in the decision-making processes affecting IT. These stakeholders form part of the organisational dimension. Elements of the COBIT 4.1 domains were selected specifically to deal with phishing threats. COBIT's guidelines of 'ensure systems security', 'monitor and evaluate internal controls' and finally 'ensure regulatory compliance' are considered applicable in addressing this linkage specific to phishing. According to COBIT 4.1, ensuring systems security is in place would satisfy the requirements for IT by maintaining the integrity of information, processing infrastructure and minimising the impact of security vulnerabilities and incidents. This is applicable not only to phishing threats but also to any security threat. Monitoring and evaluating the effectiveness of controls is an important process given the ever-changing nature of technological controls and phishing attacks. As a result, controls may have to be improved accordingly. Top-level management has a vital role to play in ensuring that the organisational IT infrastructure provides a safe, reliable and secure environment in which its employees can perform their duties. It must support information security and ensure that employees are trained to exercise their information security responsibilities. If not, this will potentially create an opportunity for phishers to target weak IT infrastructure either by exploiting technological vulnerabilities, or through employee behaviour.

5. Conclusions and Future Work

This paper examined theories and best practices that are relevant to the main relationships that influence each of the HOT elements. This provided guidance for understanding the variables that reveal gaps between each of the elements. It is evident that in all three linkages (HT, HO, and OT), the attitudes and behaviour of users influence the functioning of these linkages. Humans need to be properly educated to minimize any negative attitudes towards technology and to recognise that it is easy to use and useful for its purpose. Moreover, they need to be educated on security threats and their related risks. Humans need to be trained in using technological controls correctly to counter phishing attacks. They also need to be educated in terms of carrying out their roles and responsibilities safely in organisations; this is made possible by organisational policies and procedures. Finally, the organisation should ensure that its IT infrastructure and its associated processes are defined and managed correctly. It can be claimed that; if TAM and the agency dilemma, as described in Agency theory, together with elements of COBIT are satisfactorily introduced and maintained in an organisation, definite strides are being made towards a holistic anti-phishing framework. Accordingly, a security awareness, training and education programme will play an essential role in ensuring that these linkages form a stronger bond with the respective elements. Components of such a programme will be discussed in future work and will be evaluated by means of semi-structured interviews.

6. References

Beznosov, K., & Beznosova, O. (2007). On the imbalance of the security problem space and its expected consequences. *Information Management & Computer Security, 15*, pp. 420–431.

Cabrera, Á., Cabrera, E. F., & Barajas, S. (2001). The key role of organizational culture in a multi-system view of technology-driven change. *International Journal of Information Management, 21*, pp. 245–261.

COBIT 4.1. (2007). *COBIT 4.1 Executive Summary*. Illinois, USA: IT Governance Institute.

Davis, F. D. (1989). Perceived usefulness, perceived ease of use, and user acceptance of information technology. *MIS Quarterly, 13*, pp. 319–340.

Deloitte. (2012). *Deloitte-NASCIO Cybersecurity Study: State governments at risk: a call for collaboration and compliance.* http://www.nascio.org/events/2012Annual/documents/State-Governments-at-Risk.pdf (Accessed 20 November 2012).

Dhamija, R., Tygar, J. D., & Hearst, M. (2006). *Why phishing works*. Proceedings of the SIGCHI conference on Human Factors in computing systems, Montreal, Quebec, Canada: ACM. pp. 581–590.

Downs, J. S., Holbrook, M. B., & Cranor, L. F. (2007). *Behavioral response to phishing risk.* Proceedings of the Anti-Phishing Working Group's 2nd Annual eCrime Researchers Summit, 2007 Pittsburgh, Pennsylvania. 1299019: ACM, pp. 37-44.

Egelman, S., Cranor, L. F., & Hong, J. (2008). *You've been warned: An empirical study of the effectiveness of web browser phishing warnings*. Proceedings of the twenty-sixth annual SIGCHI conference on Human factors in computing systems. Florence, Italy: ACM. pp. 1065-1074.

Eisenhardt, K. M. (1989). Agency theory: An assessment and review. *Academy of Management Review, 14*, pp. 57–74.

Frauenstein, E. D., & Von Solms, R. (2009). Phishing: How an organisation can protect itself. *Information Security South Africa (ISSA).* Johannesburg, South Africa. pp. 253–268.

Frauenstein, E. D., & Von Solms, R. (2011). An enterprise anti-phishing framework. *Proceedings of the 7th World Conference on Information Security Education (IFIP WISE7 TC11.8),* Lucerne, Switzerland. pp. 80-88.

Herath, T., & Rao, H. R. (2009). Encouraging information security behaviors in organizations: Role of penalties, pressures and perceived effectiveness. *Decision Support Systems, 47*, pp. 154–165.

ISO/IEC 27002. (2005). Information Technology: Security techniques – Code of practice for information security management. *ISO/IEC 27002:2005.* Standards South Africa.

Jakobsson, M., Tsow, A., Shah, A., Blevis, E., & Lim, Y. K. (2007). What instills trust? A qualitative study of phishing. *Proceedings of the 11th International Conference on Financial cryptography and 1st International conference on Usable Security.* Scarborough, Trinidad and Tobago: Springer-Verlag.

Jensen, M., & Meckling, W. (1976). Theory of the firm: Managerial behavior, agency costs, and ownership structure. *Journal of Financial Economics, 3*, pp.305–360.

Kumaraguru, P., Rhee, Y., Sheng, S., Hasan, S., Acquisti, A., Cranor, L. F., & Hong, J. (2007). Getting users to pay attention to anti-phishing education: Evaluation of retention and transfer. *Proceedings of the Anti-Phishing Working Group's 2nd Annual eCrime Researchers Summit.* Pittsburgh, Pennsylvania: ACM.

Luftman, J. (2004). *Strategies for information technology governance.* Pennsylvania, USA: Idea Group (IGI Global).

Ohaya, C. (2006). Managing phishing threats in an organization. *Proceedings of the 3rd annual conference on Information security curriculum development*, 2006 Kennesaw, Georgia. 1231083: ACM. pp. 159–161.

Schlienger, T., & Teufel, S. (2003). Information security culture: From analysis to change. *Proceedings of the 3rd Annual Information Security South Africa Conference (ISSA).* Johannesburg, South Africa, pp.183–196.

Schneier, B. (2000). *Semantic attacks: The third wave of network attacks.* http://www.schneier.com/crypto-gram-0010.html#1. (Accessed 14 April 2009).

Schneier, B. (2008). The psychology of security. *Proceedings of the Cryptology in Africa 1st international conference on Progress in cryptology.* Casablanca, Morocco: Springer-Verlag.

Siponen, M. (2000). A conceptual foundation for organizational information security awareness. *Information Management & Computer Security, 8*(1), pp. 31–41.

Swanson, E. B. (1988). *Information system implementation: Bridging the gap between design and utilization.* Homewood, IL: Irwin.

Thomson, K.-L., Von Solms, R., & Louw, L. (2006). Cultivating an organizational information security culture. *Computer Fraud & Security.*

Thomson, M. E., & Von Solms, R. (1998). Information security awareness: Educating your users effectively. *Information Management & Computer Security, 6*, pp. 167–173.

Werlinger, R., Hawkey, K., & Beznosov, K. (2008). Human, organizational and technological challenges of implementing it security in organizations. *Human Aspects of Information Security and Assurance (HAISA) 2008.* Plymouth, England. pp. 1-10.

West, R. (2008). The psychology of security. *Commun. ACM, 51*, pp. 34–40.

Using Phishing Experiments and Scenario-based Surveys to Understand Security Behaviours in Practice

W.R. Flores[1], H. Holm[1], Gu. Svensson[1] and G. Ericsson[2]

[1]Department of Industrial Information and Control Systems, Royal Institute of Technology, Stockholm, Sweden
[2]Swedish National Grid, Stockholm, Sweden
e-mail: waldorf@ics.kth.se

Abstract

Threats from social engineering can cause organisations severe damage if they are not considered and managed. In order to understand how to manage those threats, it is important to examine reasons why organisational employees fall victim to social engineering. In this paper, the objective is to understand security behaviours in practice by investigating factors that may cause an individual to comply with a request posed by a perpetrator. In order to attain this objective, we collect data through a scenario-based survey and conduct phishing experiments in three organisations. The results from the experiment reveal that the degree of target information in an attack increases the likelihood that an organisational employee fall victim to an actual attack. Further, an individual's trust and risk behaviour significantly affects the actual behaviour during the phishing experiment. Computer experience at work, helpfulness and gender (females tend to be less susceptible to a generic attack than men), has a significant correlation with behaviour reported by respondents in the scenario-based survey. No correlation between the performance in the scenario-based survey and experiment was found. We argue that the result does not imply that one or the other method should be ruled out as they have both advantages and disadvantages which should be considered in the context of collecting data in the critical domain of information security. Discussions of the findings, implications and recommendations for future research are further provided.

Keywords

Social engineering, phishing, security behaviours, survey method, experiment

1. Introduction

The increased effectiveness and robustness of technical security components has made it more difficult to successfully attack computer systems using purely technical means. Many attackers have therefore started to include social means in their malicious efforts and target the humans accessing and using the computers (Applegate 2009). These types of attacks are commonly known as social engineering attacks. Social engineering is a form of deception in which an attacker attempts to deceive a victim into performing an action that benefits the attacker, e.g., click on a malicious link and install malware on their computers or reveal personal computer passwords (D Mitnick & L Simon 2002).

Social engineering is a major security threat to organizations (Barwick 2012). In order to help organizations successfully manage social engineering threats, it is crucial for researchers to understand why organizational employees are persuaded to comply with a request posed by an attacker. However, gaining access to individuals' actual behaviour is one constant challenge for researchers in the security field. Little empirical research on social engineering has included real phishing experiments due to ethical concerns related to deceiving participants without debriefing them, and even fewer have been conducted in an organizational setting to understand why organisational employees may or may not fall victim to social engineering. To the knowledge of the authors, only two papers report studies of phishing experiments in an organizational setting (the studies by Jagatic et al. (2007) and Dodgejr et al. (2007) were carried out as real phishing experiments involving university students and not organizational members). One reason for this lack of behavioural studies is that it is challenging to convince organizational managers to participate in studies in which their employees' actual behaviour is being measured. In the experiment conducted by Bakhshi et al. (2009), a phishing mail was sent out to organizational employees as a mean to provide empirical evidence of how many employees succumb to social engineering. The experiment was ceased after approximately 3.5 h. During that period of time, 23 percent of recipients were fooled by the attack. The email included factors related to how the attacker constructs the attack (e.g., trusted e-mail source, attention-grabbing subject, type of social engineering technique used) in order to understand why people fall victim to social engineering. In this paper, we refer to such factors as *external factors*. The results give insight into the problem of social engineering and how vulnerable an organization is to such an attack. No data was, however, collected on personal demographic factors and personal psychological factors to understand why organisational employees succumb to social engineering. We refer to these factors as *internal factors*. The lack of such data makes it difficult to determine personal antecedents of successful social engineering in practice. Furthermore, no information is given on how the management acted during the experiment (did they act according to normal procedures in the event of an attack?). In the study by Workman (2008) a theoretical framework was developed to empirically investigate personal antecedents of successful social engineering. The results revealed that *trust* and *fear* (among others) had significant influence on why people fall victim to social engineering. The data collection was triangulated by collecting data of subjective perceptions of behaviours and conducting objective observations. However, the information given on *external factors* that potentially could affect an individual to succumb to social engineering is limited, and no information is given on how the management acted in the event of a participant reporting his or her suspicion during the experiment. Further, the experiment was conducted over a period of six months, in which both phishing emails and pretext attacks (over the telephone) against each participant were launched two times each week. It is questionable if such an approach reflects an actual attack and using such an attack frequency may both increase the success of the attacks and the awareness of the participants as previous experience of social engineering has shown to improve an individual's resilience against social engineering (Dodgejr et al. 2007). This could potentially bias the results.

In this paper, the general purpose is to extend the understanding of security behaviours in practice by examining reasons why employees fall victim to social engineering. Specifically, we evaluate personal psychological and personal demographic antecedents of successful social engineering and analyse the influence of adding target information in an attack (important target information could include the name of the targeted organization's CIO in the email). To more fully understand the complexity of security behaviour, empirical data is collected in a multi-method approach by distributing scenario-based surveys under the false pretence of studying "micro efficiency" and conducting unannounced phishing experiments in three organizations. Scenario-based surveys have been used as a technique to assess the security readiness of organizational members in previous studies (Nohlberg 2005). The final specific purpose with this paper is therefore to evaluate if there exists any correlation between how respondents report they would behave in a given scenario in a survey and how they behave in an experiment. The rest of the paper unfolds as follows. In the next section, theory on social engineering is presented. Then, the methodology of the research conducted is presented. The section that follows outlines the results of the empirical tests based on the multi-method approach applied in three organizations. Finally, the findings are discussed and conclusions are drawn.

2. Social engineering

Social engineering consists of techniques used to manipulating people into performing actions or divulge confidential information (D Mitnick & L Simon 2002). Some attackers attempt to persuade individuals with appeals to strong human emotions such as scarcity or excitement, and others focus on adding target information to increase the effectiveness of their attacks. In this study, we want to examine reasons why people succumb to social engineering with an explicit focus on personal psychological and personal demographic factors and the influence of including target information in an attack.

2.1 Individual determinants of successful social engineering

Studies have shown that likeability and trust explain an individual's susceptibility to social engineering. The results of the study by Workman (2008) suggest that an individual that exhibits a greater trust and likeability is easier to deceive. The study also revealed that fear significantly explained why an individual fall victim to social engineering. The author showed that these relationships were significant through a combination of unannounced experiments and questionnaires. *Fear* and *trust* were therefore decided to be included in the present study. Computer self-efficacy or an individual's perception of the ability to perform a computer-related task (Moos & Azevedo 2009; Rhee et al. 2009) has been studied on several occasions and operationalized in various ways, e.g., as general knowledge of computer and as the number of hours an individual spend on a computer each week. This study operationalizes *computer self-efficacy* as the perceived overall knowledge of computers and how many years an individual has used computers in work-related situations. The influence of an individual's risk behaviour has been tested and identified to significantly influence people's susceptibility to social engineering in the study by Sheng et al. (2010). This construct is not specific to IT-related risks, but strives rather to capture general risk behaviour. Social engineering further aims at exploiting human emotions which in turn will affect a person's helpfulness. Therefore, social engineering attacks depend on the natural helpfulness of human users (Luo et al. 2011). In line with these arguments we include *risk behaviour* and *helpfulness* in the present study. To capture potential personal demographic antecedents of social engineering, we include *age* and *gender* in the survey instrument. Age and gender have been studied on previous occasions (Workman 2008; Dhamija et al. 2006; Sheng et al. 2010).

2.2 Role of target information

There are a few studies that have estimated the increased effectiveness gained through increasing the amount of target information in a phishing email. In the phishing study carried out by Jagatic et al. (2007), the value of adding target information provided by a social network was estimated. The authors conducted unannounced phishing experiments using students at their university and found that phishing using data provided by social networks gave a 72 % success rate, whereas attacks without such target information gave 16 % success rate. This study is however not very representative to the domain at large as very few phishing attacks are targeted against a specific individual rather than a larger group of individuals. Jakobsson & Ratkiewicz (2006) performed four unannounced experiments on the topic of the online auction system "rOnl". The authors studied the importance of two target specific pieces of data; whether to include the name of the recipient in the email or not ("No name" or "Good name") and the type of link provided in the email ("Good link" or ""evil" IP link" or ""Evil" Subdomain link"). The authors found that the provided link was the most important variable; the presence of recipient name in the email did not have any major influence on the success rate of an attack. This paper, as Jakobsson & Ratkiewicz (2006), aims to study social engineering attacks which are representative to the attack type in general. As a consequence a very important factor is that the attacks need to be automated to some degree. This study utilizes two types of methods to assess susceptibility to social engineering attacks: scenario-based surveys and phishing emails, and these are categorized as one fully automated generic attack (in our case; an attack that only require an email address) and one attack that is targeted against Enterprises in Sweden. The attacks are further described in Section 3. The actual scenarios in the survey and emails used in the experiment can be obtained from the corresponding author.

3. Methodology

As there are characteristic differences between self-perceptions of behaviour and actual behaviour, it is preferable to observe behaviour when possible. However, since all possible behaviours related to social engineering cannot be observed, observation alone is also incomplete (Workman 2008). In order to increase the understanding of complex human behaviour related to social engineering, this study combine these two data collection methods and thus are able to assess how well these two methods go together and if any relations between the results obtained from these two methods exist.

The studies were carried out from April to December 2012. Four different types of tools were used to collect data during this period: scenario-based surveys, experiments, journals and follow-up interviews. In order to conduct phishing experiments, the management of the three organizations was first approached to get their approval and support for the study. The Chief Executive Officer (CEO) of each organization was notified of the study and the IT manager from each organization took part in designing the study and collecting data. These individuals were also the only employees aware of the study. The nature of the study is such that details about the organizations cannot be presented, but a short description is given as follows: The first organisation has 11 full-time employees (not counting the CEO and IT manager). The company's main focus is in the human resource field in where they conduct employee surveys followed by management coaching and quality improvements. Most of their clients are in the public sector and for the sake of their clients integrity they perceive information security to be important. The second organisation has 32 full-time employees, and the third organization has 49 employees (not counting the CEO and IT manager). Both organisations are in the electrical power domain and the inherent need for security in a these companies is therefore high. All employees of each organization were chosen to be included in the study to maximize the sample size and thus having 92 participants in the study.

3.1 Scenario-based Survey

A smoke-screen approach was used as previous research has argued that it is more effective to capture the employee's security awareness if they are not aware of their awareness being assessed (Nohlberg 2005). This is because the respondents might act differently if they knew that their awareness (or possible lack of) was being assessed. Thus, we wanted to examine if users have a spontaneous awareness of common social engineering cons. The context of the survey was the need to determine how effective an organisation's employees are in the process of performing small work-related tasks during a typically day at work.

The data collection phase started by the IT managers sending out an email and informing their employees about a study in "micro efficiency" and encouraging them to answer a survey related to this study. In line with the purpose of applying a smoke screen approach, three of the scenarios were general scenarios and three where security-related. We attempted to construct scenarios that reflect three actual attacks: update of a well-known software for displaying, printing and managing documents (scenario generic attack), update of the organisation's security software (scenario targeted attack) and acquire of computer password (scenario password). Each scenario was followed by a question to find out what the respondent would do in the outlined scenario on a 7-point Likert scale from 1 to 7 with three fixed points (1: I'll do what I'm asked to do instantly; 4: I hesitate and ask if I can come back to the requester; 7: I completely refuse to do what I'm asked to do). The survey was followed by questions that were aimed to measure the independent variables. To avoid raising any suspicion among the respondents, the questions that were related to measuring the independent variables were explained to be general diagnostic questions and were described to not be related to the scenarios. These dependent variables were measured with single items. Single items are useful and effective for their practical advantages like ease of application and the low costs associated with surveys in which they are used. Further, Bergkvist & Rossiter (2007) found that, in their study, there were no difference in the predictive validity of the multiple-item and single-item measures. The items that were extracted from the study by Workman

(2008) were chosen based on highest loading to their construct and as the constructs were identified to have high composite reliability, the items within the same construct measure the same thing. All items except age, gender and computer experience at work, were measured on a 7-point Likert scale from 1 (Strongly disagree) to 7 (Strongly agree). Gender was used as a dichotomous variable with two states; 1 (Male) and 0 (Female). The items are presented in table 1.

Construct	Item
Trust	Friendly people are usually trustworthy.
Fear	I believe it is important to follow the chain of command.
Risk behaviour	I prefer excitement before a calm and safe every-day.
Computer self-efficacy	I consider myself relatively experienced and skilled with computers.
Helpfulness	I like to help other people.
Computer experience at work	How many years have you worked using a desk-top computer?
Gender	Are you male or female?
Age	How old are you?

Table 1: Survey items

To address common methods bias (CMB) we counterbalanced the order of questions in the questionnaire to discourage participants from figuring out the relationship between the dependent (scenarios) and independent variables that we were trying to establish. Further, the respondent's anonymity reduced the likelihood of bias caused by social desirability or respondent acquiescence (P. M. Podsakoff et al. 2003).

3.2 Experimental design

Two experiments were carried out. Their base scenario was the same. However, the content of the emails were significantly different; the first email being a generic large-scale phishing email, and the second a phishing email with specific information about the target organisation inluded. A pilot study was used to verify that all emails were received by their specified recipients, that the web server was reachable, and that the binary could send data through the firewall. An SMTP server (Postfix) and an HTTP server (Apache) were set up at the research department. The attack was carried out as follows. The SMTP server at the research department sends a "malicious" email to each employee. Every email is outfitted with a unique link to the HTTP server at the research department. An employee clicks on the link in the email and reaches the HTTP server at the research department. The HTTP server was set up to: (i) log user information through a PHP script, and (ii) to automatically serve the "malicious" binary to anyone browsing its contents. The HTTP server sends the "malicious" binary to the employee. This binary did not install anything on the system – it served as a one-time SMTP client. When executed it read the name of the system and the logged-in user, and sent this information to the email account of the conducting researcher (through the mentioned SMTP server at the research department). When the binary had read the system variables and sent these to the researcher it abruptly ended, giving the end-user an error message. The binary also had the correct product icon, but with no specified publisher. The researcher is notified that the binary has been executed, when it was executed, whom that executed it, and on which system that it was executed.

The attacks in the experiment reflected two scenarios outlined in the distributed survey (generic and targeted attack). The rationale was to enable evaluation of any correlation between how respondents report they would behave in a given scenario and how the behave in the experiment. The first experiment concerned an update of well-known software for displaying, printing and managing documents which was employed on all computers in the enterprise. In this paper, the name of the software is Knylo Reader (the name is obfuscated through ROT10). This product is in the enterprise updated through a service which is installed along with the application. This attack is not targeted at any particular user or organization; from an attackers perspective a recipient is the only information that is required. The domain (www.knldownloads.com) was used to point to the "malicious" HTTP server at the research department. The email was spoofed from support@knylo.com and the user was requested to download the latest version of their software (version 11, which was not released yet at the time of the study). The content of the email was written for the exercise but builds significantly on previous actual phishing attacks using the same product. Furthermore, it was qualitatively reviewed by five external researchers.

The second mail concerns a targeted attack against enterprises in Sweden. The context of the email involves the updating of the enterprise's antivirus software with a temporary add-on as the current antivirus version does not cover the virus that has infected some of the organisation's computer systems. The user is requested to click on a link and update the current antivirus software with the temporary add-on. The email was spoofed from the IT managers' actual email addresses. The whole email was written in grammatically correctly Swedish. This email was specifically written for the experiment and reviewed by five external researchers. However, it was not specifically customized for the studied enterprise, but rather Swedish enterprises in general. In practice there was no need to update the antivirus software at the enterprise. Furthermore, this type of actions is carried out from a central IT-administration, and the IT-managers don't pose any requests of this kind through e-mail. The email was also composed without knowledge regarding how the IT managers typically expressed themselves. As a consequence, the email differed significantly from the style of actual emails by the IT managers. This should serve to make the results of the attack representative to the population at large. The second experiment as such exhibit two critical differences compared to the first experiment: (i) the attacker has to be able to write in Swedish (or consult a third party, e.g., an online service, to translate it) and (ii) the attacker has to find the email to the IT managers of the targeted organisations and be able to relate those individuals to all others in the targeted organisations. In practice, this type of targeted attack is much more effort-demanding than the generic attack. However, such information can be easily accessible; especially for small enterprises. For example, present on the company website or on social media sites such as LinkedIn.

3.3 Analysis Methodology

In order to analyse the relationship between the individual factors and the dependent variable, point-biserial correlation was used. The point-biserial correlation coefficient is a special case of Pearson correlation and can handle dependent variables that are operationlised as scale variables and dichotomous variables. For the dichotomous variable the values typically are 1 (presence) and 0 (absence) (Glass & Hopkins 1995). Thus, this analysis technique fits the purpose of study and we used susceptibility to social engineering (i.e. successful attack) as a dichotomous variable with two states: 1 (Yes) and 0 (No).

4. Results

4.1. Survey results

The survey was sent to the 92 participants of the study. One reminder was sent to non-responding participant after one week. Overall, 54 respondents (59 %) completed the survey. Descriptive results are displayed in table 2. The results indicate that a targeted attack (ScTA) would be most effective and acquiring passwords (ScPW) would be most difficult from an attacker's point of view. Notable are the extremely high mean value of the ScTA and the absolute value of the standard deviation (due to several outliers). A box plot for the descriptive results was analysed and the removal of the outliers yielded a mean value of 7.0. However, we decided to keep the outliers in the descriptive results (presented in table 2) to display the fact that some respondents actually did not report that they would instantly do what they're asked to in a targeted attack.

	Min	Max	Mean	Std. Deviation	N
ScGA	1	7	4.630	2.192	54
ScTA	1	7	6.593	1.125	54
ScPW	1	7	3.926	2.073	54

Table 2: Descriptive survey results

4.2. Experiment

An overview of the results from the phishing experiment can be seen in Table 3. Eight out of 92 recipients, or 8.7 %, clicked the "malicious" link in the generic attack. Three recipients also executed the "malicious" binary. Adding target information in the attack significantly increased the number of employees clicking on the "malicious" link. In the targeted attack, 29 out of 92 recipients, or 31.5 %, clicked the "malicious" link. Six of these individuals executed the "malicious" binary. One individual who executed the binary during the first experiment also executed the binary during the second experiment. Furthermore, all of these individuals executed the binary several times. However, none of the employees executed the binary on more than a single account and system. Nevertheless, these systems could in theory have been more or less vulnerable to the attack during these different executions. During both experiments (the second created a larger amount of activities at the organisations) the IT managers received reports from security-aware employees. Since the experiment was supposed to be representative to an actual attack in practice and we wanted to capture management behaviour during this event, the IT-managers were told to act as they normally do in an event of a security attack. Therefore the experiment was ceased by the IT-manager sending out a warning about the emails, after approximately 20 minutes in the first attack and after 10 minutes in the second attack. However, there were still employees trying to access the malicious website after the official warning (and knowing that it in fact was malicious). The last attempt to access the malicious website occurred 20 hours after the generic attack and 24 hours after the targeted attack. We can think of two possible reasons that explain this phenomenon: (i) curiosity and (ii) not knowing the dangers involved when browsing malicious websites.

Click link	No.	Percent
Generic attack	8	8.7
Targeted attack	29	31.5
Execute binary		
Generic attack	3	3.3
Targeted attack	6	6.5

Table 3: Overall results from the phishing experiments

4.3. Individual factors explaining susceptibility to social engineering

One of our purposes was to evaluate individual factors that explain why organisational employees succumb to social engineering. Due to the limited sample size associated with the execution of the binary, the analysis was based on individuals clicking on the "malicious" link. Further, we could only use data from the respondents that actually completed the distributed survey (n=54). The results are presented in table 4. ExSA refers to successful attack during the experiment, while ScGA, ScTA and ScPW refer to the three scenarios outlined in the survey described in section 3.1: general attack, targeted attack and password. The statistical results reveal that *computer experience at work*, *gender* (females tend to be less susceptible to a generic attack than men), and *helpfulness* has a significant correlation with behaviour reported by respondents in the scenario-based survey, while *trust* and *risk behaviour* significantly affects the actual behaviour during the phishing experiments.

	ExSA	ScGA	ScTA	ScPW	N
Trust	.285*	.092	-.031	-.017	54
Fear	-.070	.096	-.106	.037	54
Risk behaviour	.305*	.079	-.134	-.004	54
Computer self-efficacy	-.010	.210	.008	.018	54
Helpfulness	-.094	.119	-.018	.291*	54
Computer experience at work	.003	-.285*	.204	.087	54
Gender	.043	-.380**	-.108	-.095	54
Age	.144	-.176	.223	.087	54

Table 4: Significance of individual antecedents

Notes: * indicates statistically significant at $p < 0.05$; and ** at $p < 0.01$.

4.4. Combined results

The final purpose was to examine if there exists any correlation between the results from the self-report study (how respondents report they would behave in a given scenario in a survey) and the observations (their actual behaviour in an experiment). We found no correlation between these variables. A correlation matrix of nonsignificant values is presented in table 5 to illustrate the relations between the three social engineering scenarios in the survey (ScGA, ScTA, ScPW) and the actual social engineering attack (ExSA). To examine how the participants reacted to the experiment, we distributed a follow-up survey and when possible, conducted semi-structured follow-up interviews. Overall, the participants perceived the study to be important, had positive feelings about the study and that the study had increased their interest of information security in general and social engineering in particular.

	ExSA	ScGA	ScTA	ScPW
ExSA	1	-.071	.026	-.049
ScGA	-.071	1	-.032	.015
ScTA	.026	-.032	1	.205
ScPW	-.049	.015	.205	1

Table 5: Pearson correlation coefficients for cross correlations

5. Discussions and Conclusions

Social engineering is a major security threat to organizations. One explanation for the threat is the increased effectiveness and robustness of technical security components which has made it more difficult to successfully attack computer systems using purely technical means. A way of compromising information security is then to manipulate computer users into installing malware on their computer or revealing their passwords. In order to understand how to manage social engineering threats, this study tries to understand security behaviours in practice by investigating factors that may cause an individual to fall victim to social engineering. In doing so, this study makes important contributions to the body of knowledge on social engineering in general and reason why organizational employees fall victim to those types of attacks in particular. First, this, to the best of our knowledge, is the first study that has combined a smoke screen survey approach with phishing attacks that are representative to the attack type in general (the attacks are automated to some degree) when collecting data on security behaviours. Second, the results reveal that the degree of target information in an attack increases the likelihood that an organisational employee fall victim to an attack. This results is in line with the results obtained by Jakobsson & Ratkiewicz (2006) and Jagatic et al. (2007). Therefore, we argue that organisations should consider the potential benefits from making enterprise-specific information such as employees' email addresses and titles of organisational members publically available, against the risk that this target information can be collected by an attacker to both spoof e-mail addresses and to instil trust in organisational members. In the end, it's up to the organisation to balance the need to enable the business against the need to secure information assets.

Third, our study has identified that *computer experience at work, gender* (females tend to be less susceptible to a generic attack than men), and *helpfulness* showed to have a significant correlation with behaviour reported by respondents in the scenario-based survey, while *trust* and *risk behaviour* significantly affects the actual behaviour during the phishing experiments. These findings indicate that a practical implication could be that organizations should include techniques that are used by social engineers to instil trust and encourage helpfulness and risk behaviour in their security awareness programs.

Our study revealed that surveys and observations capture different factors that explain security behaviours. However, we acknowledge the challenges in collecting data in the critical domain of information security and thus do not rule out one or the other method as we believe they have both advantages and disadvantages. Some might argue that observations capture the actual behaviour. We argue that using observations, exclusively, cannot fully capture the human complex behaviour. For instance, the follow-up survey and interviews revealed that there were occasions in which participants were encouraged and convinced by their colleagues to click on the link. Obviously, this makes it difficult to say if the respondent's actual susceptibility to the attack was measured when appeals to social norms might influence the results. We acknowledge the difficulties in measuring security behaviour and suggest that a deeper understanding of this phenomenon is required, recommending further use of a multiple method approach when attempting to measure security behaviours.

The ethical dilemma related to conducting social engineering experiments in practice makes it rather challenging to recruit participant organisations. Therefore our conclusions are based on relatively few samples. This makes it difficult to generalize the results gained from this study to the domain at large. Nevertheless, it is important to recognize that this study provides insight to properties never before studied. Also, the sample size is comparable to other phishing experiments using unaware respondents (e.g., Jakobsson & Ratkiewicz (2006)). A further limitation is that the scenario-based survey and two experiments were conducted on the same sample of respondents – it is possible that the results of the second experiment are biased from the first. However, there is strong reason to believe that this is not the case: (i) the first experiment (Knylo Reader) was launched 2 months after the survey had been completed and is similar to other spam that is frequently received by employees at the enterprise, and (ii) the second attack was launched approximately three months after the first attack. Finally, we did not spoof a legal website or constructed our own "malicious" website for the study. After the binary had read the system variables and sent these to the researcher it abruptly ended, giving the end-user an error message. We can only speculate the difference in effectiveness if we had spoofed a legitimate website or constructed our own website that serves the purpose of the study.

6. References

Applegate, S.D., 2009. Social Engineering: Hacking the Wetware! *Information Security Journal: A Global Perspective*, 18(1), pp.40–46.

Bakhshi, T., Papadaki, M. & Furnell, S., 2009. Social engineering: assessing vulnerabilities in practice. *Information Management & Computer Security*, 17(1), pp.53–63.

Barwick, H., 2012. Social engineering, big data top security priorities for 2013: Gartner. *Computerworld.* Available at: http://www.computerworld.com.au/article/441539/social_engineering_big_data_top_security_priorities_2013_gartner_/ [Accessed January 10, 2013].

Bergkvist, L. & Rossiter, J.R., 2007. The Predictive Validity of Multiple-Item Versus Single-Item Measures of the Same Constructs. *Journal of Marketing Research*, 44(2), pp.175–184.

D Mitnick, K. & L Simon, W., 2002. *The Art of Deception: Controlling the Human Element of Security*, Indianapolis, Indiana: Wiley Publishing.

Dodgejr, R., Carver, C. & Ferguson, A., 2007. Phishing for user security awareness. *Computers & Security*, 26(1), pp.73–80.

Glass, G. V. & Hopkins, K.D., 1995. *Statistical Methods in Education and Psychology* 3rd ed., Allyn & Bacon.

Jagatic, T.N. et al., 2007. Social phishing. *Communications of the ACM*, 50(10), pp.94–100.

Jakobsson, M. & Ratkiewicz, J., 2006. Designing ethical phishing experiments. In *Proceedings of the 15th international conference on World Wide Web - WWW '06*. New York, New York, USA: ACM Press, p. 513.

Luo, X. et al., 2011. Social Engineering: The Neglected Human Factor for Information Security Management. *Information Resources Management Journal*, 24(3), pp.1–8.

Moos, D.C. & Azevedo, R., 2009. Learning With Computer-Based Learning Environments: A Literature Review of Computer Self-Efficacy. *Review of Educational Research*, 79(2), pp.576–600.

Nohlberg, M., 2005. Social Engineering Audits Using Anonymous Surveys – Conning the Users in Order to Know if They Can Be Conned. In *Proceedings of the 4th Security Conference*. Las Vegas, USA.

Podsakoff, P.M. et al., 2003. Common method biases in behavioral research: a critical review of the literature and recommended remedies. *The Journal of applied psychology*, 88(5), pp.879–903.

Sheng, S. et al., 2010. Who falls for phish? In *Proceedings of the 28th international conference on Human factors in computing systems - CHI '10*. New York, New York, USA: ACM Press, p. 373.

Workman, M., 2008. Wisecrackers: A theory-grounded investigation of phishing and pretext social engineering threats to information security. *Journal of the American Society for Information Science and Technology*, 59(4), pp.662–674.

Developing and Testing a Visual Hash Scheme

M. M. Olembo, T. Kilian, S. Stockhardt, A. Hülsing and M. Volkamer

Center for Advanced Security Research Darmstadt
Technische Universität Darmstadt
e-mail : {maina.olembo, timo.kilian, simon.stockhardt, andreas.huelsing,
melanie.volkamer}@cased.de

Abstract

Users find comparing long meaningless strings of alphanumeric characters difficult, yet they have to carry out this task when comparing cryptographic hash values for https certificates and PGP keys, or in the context of electronic voting. Visual hashes - where users compare images rather than strings - have been proposed as an alternative. With the visual hashes available in literature, however, people are unable to sufficiently distinguish more than 30 bits. Obviously, this does not provide adequate security against collision attacks. Our goal is to improve the situation: a visual hash scheme was developed, evaluated through pilot user studies and improved iteratively, leading to CLPS, which encodes 60 distinguishable bits using Colours, Patterns and Shapes. In the final user study, participants attained an average accuracy rate of 97% when comparing two visual hash images, with one placed above the other. CLPS was further tested in two follow-up studies, simulating https certificate validation and verifying in remote electronic voting. The results of this work and their implications for practical applications of visual hash schemes are discussed.

Keywords

Visual hash, Usability, Security, Hash function

1. Introduction

Cryptographic hash functions are widely used to guarantee integrity and provide authentication on the Internet. Different use-cases are available including verifying the authenticity of https certificates and PGP encryption keys as well as verifying the proper behaviour of an electronic voting system. In most use-cases, it is necessary to compare two hash values with each other; one is presented on the screen and the other one is available on paper. For example, in the case of https certificates, some certificate owners (like banks) distribute the hash values of their certificates (also called fingerprints) in print media to their clients. If the clients visit the corresponding webpage they can compare the printed fingerprint with the one displayed by the web browser. In many verifiable electronic voting systems, voters are asked to write down the hash value of their encrypted vote in order to verify the integrity of the voting software by later (in the vote casting process) comparing this hash value to a displayed one. In all the use-cases, hash values are represented by long strings (the length depends on the hash function and the encoding applied to the hash value). As a result, users are asked to compare long strings that hold little meaning to them. Consequently, they are not very likely to perform this task which decreases the security of the applications dramatically. In addition, users are known to be poor at this task (Perrig and Song, 1999).

Visual hashes offer an alternative, with studies as early back as Shepard (1967) showing that people perform better at interacting with images compared to text. With existing schemes proposed in literature, people were unable to sufficiently distinguish more than 30 bits. However visual hash schemes need to encode more bits to provide adequate security against collision attacks. Our objective is to improve the situation by developing a visual hash scheme where more bits can be distinguished by people, i.e., that provides a higher level of entropy in practical use.

The contribution of this work - CLPS - is a visual hash scheme encoding 60 bits using Colours, Patterns and Shapes. When tested in a user study where images were placed above and below each other for comparison, the average accuracy rate on images with obvious differences (easy pairs) was 98.8% and 94.6% on images with no differences or hard-to-detect differences (hard pairs), i.e. users could sufficiently distinguish two hash values. The combined average accuracy rate for both easy and hard pairs was 97%. CLPS was further simulated in realistic scenarios and tested in two follow-up studies: in verifiability in remote electronic voting where participants achieved an accuracy rate of 73.4% on hard pairs, and in https certificate validation, where they achieved an average accuracy rate of 78.6% for hard pairs. We discuss the implications of these results for practical applications of visual hashes.

2. Related work

Visual hashes were first explored by Perrig and Song (1999) using images generated from a computer program Random Art available at (Gallery of Random Art, 2013). Random Art was initially developed to automatically generate artistic images. It takes a binary string as input from which an image is generated randomly. Since then some more visual hash schemes have been proposed and studied in literature: Flag (Ellison and Dohrmann, 2003) and T-Flag (Lin *et al.* 2009).

Hsiao *et al.* (2009) carried out an online user study of textual and all three visual hash schemes along with their own proposal called Flag Extension. The textual schemes that were tested are Base32 (Josefsson, 2006), English words (Ford *et al.* 2006), and Chinese, Japanese, and Korean characters. To enable comparison between these schemes, the entropy was set to a value between 22 and 28 bits. Easy and hard image pairs were constructed for each scheme, where the authors defined an easy pair as containing two images that were equal, or obviously different, while hard pairs contained two images with hard-to-detect differences. Participants performed the best on accuracy rates and response times for Base32, Random Art, T-Flag and Flag Extension. Results from the work by Hsiao *et al.* (2009) are shown in Table 1.

Hsiao *et al.* (2009) argue that Random Art, Flag, and T-Flag can only guarantee limited entropy as the only way to increase the number of encoded bits is to use more colours, which makes the resulting images harder to distinguish. Thus, the number of encoded bits would increase but the level of entropy would not increase in practical use. For this reason, it seems necessary to come up with a new proposal to achieve a higher level of entropy for practical use, i.e., people are able to distinguish any two images that encode two different hash values.

Category	Encoded bits	Easy Pairs		Hard Pairs	
		Accuracy (%)	Time (s)	Accuracy (%)	Time (s)
Base32	25	97	3.39	86	3.51
Random Art	24*	98	4.77	94	3.21
T-Flag	24	98	6.31	85	5.30
Flag Extension	24	98	3.93	88	4.02

Table 1: Average accuracy rate and response time results from Hsiao *et al.* (2009).

*Note: the authors estimated the perceptual entropy of Random Art. Here, we provide the maximum number of bits that could be encoded.

3. Scheme development and pilot studies

In this section we discuss how the visual hash scheme was developed iteratively, describe how participants were recruited and their tasks, and summarize findings from the pilot user studies.

3.1. Original visual hash idea

People are known to be good at identifying geometrical shapes, patterns and colours (Reynolds, 1972). As a result, we decided to base our proposal for a new visual hash scheme on colours, patterns and shapes. An object is therefore defined by its shape and the pattern and colour it is filled with.

A wide range of possible values for the parameters were selected through several iterative discussions between the co-authors as well as with other colleagues leading to the following selection: four patterns (2 bits), 32 shapes (5 bits), two positions (up or down – 1 bit) and four objects in one image. Additionally, we used a colour contrast analyser and selected eight colours (3 bits) that can easily be distinguished by humans, taking into account colour-blindness. This resulted in 11 bits per object and 44 bits for an image. Four characters from a Base32 alphabet (5 bits per character, leading to 20 bits in total) were added to the image to further increase the number of encoded bits. Base32 had obtained good results in the study from Hsiao *et al.* (2009). In total, we can encode 64 bits with this approach.

3.2. Evaluation of the visual hash

We evaluated and improved this approach based on lab user studies, which allowed the participants to be observed. Timing was important as response time data was the usability measure applied to evaluate the effectiveness of the visual hash scheme. As such, the lab studies were useful in ensuring that the comparison task was carried out in a reasonable amount of time. The methodology used was the same in all user studies during the development as well as for the final evaluation (see Section 4). This methodology is described and justified in this subsection.

Hard and easy pairs: For the studies, we designed easy and hard pairs of images, where an easy pair consisted of two images that were obviously different, i.e., in which many parameters changed, while a hard pair consisted of two images that were either equal or had slight differences between them, i.e., parameters were changed to values that were visually close (for example, changing 'Z' to '2'). Note that this definition differs from that given in Hsiao *et al.* (2009). In our work, equal pairs are considered as hard pairs since all, or close to all, parameters of the pairs would have to be compared by the user to determine whether or not they were equal.

Users' tasks and methodology to collect and analyse the data: A PowerPoint presentation was developed to display the image pairs on each slide, to allow participants to answer whether the images were equal or not, to store the answers given per slide, and to automatically deduce the participants' accuracy rate and response times and store this result into an Excel data sheet for analysis. Visual Basic for Applications (VBA) scripts were written for this purpose.

The first page of the presentation gave an explanation of the study and the task that the participants were to carry out. It also showed an example of the images for comparison and explained what could differ. On the second slide, participants entered demographic data, specifying their age, gender, and level of comfort with computers. They could then begin the interactive part of the study. The slides were displayed randomly; each slide contained two images, one displayed above, or next to, the other, depending on the study. A participant then had to decide if the images were identical or different and pushed a green 'tick' button to indicate that the images matched, or a red 'cross' button to indicate that the images did not match. When participants had gone through all the slides, they commented on their perception of the study on one slide of the presentation, after which their results were displayed, showing them the number of images they had correctly identified to be equal or different. Examples of the PowerPoint slides used in the pilot studies are shown in Figure 1(a) and (b).

While we collected three usability measures - effectiveness (accuracy rate), efficiency (response time), and satisfaction (users' subjective responses) – only a few participants gave subjective responses on their perception of the visual hash scheme. As a result, we only report accuracy rate and response time results. While high accuracy rates are important, they are especially important for hard pairs as they indicate the extent to which participants can successfully distinguish differences in visual hashes, showing the scheme to be useful for practical use, e.g. when collision attacks are attempted.

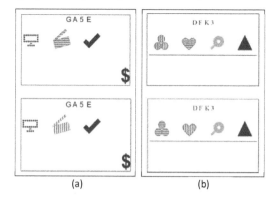

(a)   (b)

Figure 1: Image pairs in the pilot user studies: (a) original idea with images above and below each other, (b) original idea extended with horizontal partitioning line

Study Participants: They were administrative employees from a company, and students and employees from a research institute and a university. German was used for the studies, and participants were either German native speakers, or proficient in German (i.e., used it for work and study). They were verbally invited to participate in the user study. No compensation was offered. Participants were informed that their task was to compare images, and they were to indicate if what they viewed was the same or different. They were not trained on the image comparison task.

3.3. Findings of pilot user studies and scheme improvement

The original idea was tested with 16 participants (see Figure 1(a)). Eleven participants did not notice that the objects in the hard pairs moved from the 'up' to 'down' position and nine participants did not detect a change from the 'down' to 'up' position. Additionally, seven participants were unable to distinguish between dotted and horizontal-wavy patterns (not shown in the figure). In order to improve the situation we inserted a horizontal partitioning line as proposed by participants of the first pilot study. Furthermore, we replaced wavy line patterns with straight ones instead.

This new version (see Figure 1(b)) was tested with 16 new participants. Here seven participants did not distinguish the first object changing from the 'down' to 'up' position. Additionally, six participants were unable to distinguish the two centre objects switching between the 'up' and 'down' position and vice versa. As the partitioning line did not sufficiently improve the errors regarding the position parameter, we discarded the position parameter (4 bits as each object in the visual hash used one bit for position), and retained only the colours, shapes and pattern parameters for the final visual hash scheme - CLPS - encoding 60 bits (see Figure 2).

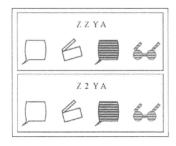

Figure 2: CLPS image pair

4. CLPS and Base32

A study was carried out to evaluate participants' accuracy rate and response time results with CLPS and Base 32, both encoding 60 bits. Participants performed well with Base32 in Hsiao *et al.* (2009), motivating inclusion of Base32 in this study. Two groups of participants were recruited. One group interacted with CLPS, and the second group with Base32. The study design was the same as for the pilot studies. The study design and results of the user study are reported in this section.

Study Design: The easy pair images in this study were obviously different image pairs, while the hard pair images were either equal or contained one or two differences in them. Ten slides had equal images, five slides had obviously different images and ten slides had slight differences in the images as follows: two slides with shapes changing, two slides with letters changing ('Z' to '2'; '5' to 'S'), two slides with colours changing (black to grey; turquoise to blue), and four slides with patterns changing. This selection was based on parameters where participants performed poorly in the pilot user studies. Image pairs were displayed randomly for every participant. There were 30 participants and the average age was 34.7 years. The youngest and oldest participants were 24 and 43 years old, respectively.

In the Base32 study, the text for comparison was 12 characters long (5 bits encoded into one Base32 character, thus, 60 bits in total). There were ten slides with equal alpha-numeric characters, five slides with obviously different ones, and ten slides with slight differences (e.g., one character changing, such as, 4NNKV4XTLPB7S and 4NNKV4XTRPB7S). Image pairs were displayed randomly for every participant. This study had 35 participants, who had an average age of 27.7 years. The youngest and oldest participants were 19 and 63 years old, respectively.

Results: Participants took slightly less time to compare CLPS images than they did to compare Base32 characters for both easy pairs (6.3s for CLPS and 6.9s for Base32), and hard pairs (4.6s for CLPS and 6.3s for Base32), showing participants to be more efficient at CLPS comparison than Base32. Additionally, the average accuracy rate for easy pairs was comparable to that of Base32 (98.8% - CLPS and 99.6% - Base32), and better than Base32 for the hard pairs (94.6% - CLPS and 89.2% - Base32). A high accuracy rate in hard pairs is important as it shows the extent to which participants can successfully distinguish differences, e.g., where collision attacks are attempted.

The results from this study show CLPS to be a viable visual hash scheme, with acceptable accuracy rate and response time results. Therefore, CLPS was tested in follow-up studies simulating realistic use: verifiability in Helios (Adida, 2008), a verifiable Internet voting system, and https certificate validation. These two studies and the accompanying results are reported in Sections 5 and 6.

5. Study simulating verifiability in Helios

This study was designed to evaluate the use of visual hashes in the Helios Internet voting system (Karayumak *et al.* 2011) to perform the so-called cast as intended verification.

Study design: The easy pair images in this study had obvious differences in the parameters, while the hard pair images were either equal or designed to have one or two differences in one parameter, i.e., colour, pattern or shape. This selection was motivated by the results of participants' performance with CLPS reported in Section 4. Thus we selected parameters that participants made errors in. Image pairs were displayed randomly for every participant.

Participants first saw a CLPS image displayed on a PowerPoint slide. They were asked a brief, distracting question on a second slide, for example, 'What is your favourite ice-cream?', and provided with multiple-choice responses. The third slide displayed to participants contained another visual hash image and participants indicated if it was similar to or different from the first one they had seen. This process simulated the Helios interface, where voters would see a hash value (first visual hash), select an option from several available options to carry out the verification process (distracting question), and then view the results of the verification, determining whether a second hash value displayed in a new window (second visual hash) matched the first one they had seen previously. Each participant repeated this process five times. Forty-five participants took part in the study. They had an average age of 26.8 years. The youngest and oldest participants were 19 and 57 years old, respectively.

Results: Participants had an average accuracy rate of 96.7% for easy pairs and took an average of 18.9s, while the accuracy rate was 73.4% for hard pairs where they took an average of 20.9s. CLPS is thus seen as a promising alternative for practical use in this use-case given the results obtained and considering the results from related work shown in Table 1.

Colour and pattern parameters proved problematic for participants, with 18 and 11 errors being made, respectively. Improvements will be investigated in future work, along with changes to the images to aid participants' recollection. We anticipate this will improve performance for practical use even further.

6. Study simulating https certificate validation

A study was carried out with participants comparing hash values for https certificates represented using CLPS.

In a pre-test, with 30 participants, we identified which image pairs to use for the study. As no errors were made by participants in the easy image pairs (containing obvious differences), we decided to only evaluate equal image pairs and images containing slight differences. Both of these are defined as hard pairs in Section 3.2. We therefore refer to them as equal pairs and slight-difference pairs in this section, where the study design and results of the user study are reported.

Study design: Three out of eight image pairs were equal, while the remaining five pairs were slight-difference pairs (for example, swapping one character). Participants were given eight different letters from well-known online environments, specifically online stores, social networking sites, and banks. The letters contained instructions for participants to verify the hash values of the https certificates. The hash values represented with CLPS for each website were displayed on a PowerPoint presentation, and the image pairs were displayed randomly for every participant.

As participants clicked through the presentation, they would pick up the letter fitting to the certificate on the screen and carry out the comparison. An example of a comparison simulation for Facebook is shown in Figure 3. Thirty participants took part in the study. Their average age was 38.8 years. The youngest and oldest participants were 20 and 58 years old, respectively.

Figure 3: Comparing CLPS image for Facebook

Results: Participants had an average accuracy rate of 100% and an average response time of 16.6s for equal pairs, while with slight-difference pairs, the average accuracy rate was 78.6% and the average response time was 13.7s.

Fifteen participants made errors when the line pattern in the fourth object in the image changed from vertical to horizontal. Colour was also problematic for participants, with 12 participants making errors with this parameter. The causes of these errors and possible solutions will be investigated in future work.

From these results, as well as those reported in related work (shown in Table 1), CLPS is seen as promising for further investigation in future work for this use-case. Since participants received no training in the comparison task, and as https certificates change infrequently, we anticipate that improvements in accuracy rates in practical use can be achieved, especially for hard pairs.

7. Discussion and Future Work

The practical use of CLPS and its scalability and security are discussed in this section.

7.1. Practical use of CLPS

We have shown CLPS to be a viable visual hash scheme, achieving comparable average accuracy results to those of Hsia *et al.* (2009) yet also attaining higher entropy in user studies. In applying CLPS to practical use, the results obtained in both the user study simulating https certificate validation and that simulating verifiability in Helios suggest that visual hashes are of particular relevance for both use-cases.

Since https certificates change infrequently in many cases on the Internet, users can easily notice any introduced changes to a visual hash they interact and become familiar with over a period of time. However, the visual hash value should be displayed e.g., in the first few seconds when a user visits a web page. In future work training participants on the comparison task will be investigated as we anticipate that this will improve accuracy on slight-difference pairs and speed up the comparison time. A realistic scenario will be implemented, where participants visit a web page several times and the visual hash is changed completely or slightly. As users are likely to get accustomed to this over time and perhaps no longer carry out the comparison, means of avoiding this also need to be evaluated.

In the study simulating verifiability in Helios, users had to recall images after viewing them for a short period of time, affecting their accuracy rate on hard pairs. For future work, we will explore whether using a story in the visual hash images generated in this work, will help participants better remember the images, and speed up the response time.

7.2. Scalability of CLPS

CLPS can be used to encode 60 bits and achieve the same amount of entropy. This is a first step towards a higher security level, but it is still not enough to guarantee collision resistance in practice. CLPS is however easily scalable: for this initial proposal, we used only a limited number of varying colours, patterns and shapes. We identified that colours and certain patterns are problematic for users to distinguish. The current results suggest that we can increase the number of parameters that were not problematic for users to some extent, e.g., shapes and objects, while the entropy is increased by the same amount, as long as the distinguishability by people does not shrink faster, i.e., the entropy still grows.

8. References

Adida, B. (2008), "Helios: Web-based open-audit voting", *Proceedings of the 17th Symposium on Security*, San Jose, CA, 2008, pp. 335 - 348.

Gallery of Random Art, (2013), http://www.random-art.org, (Accessed 28 March 2013)

Ellison, C., and Dohrmann, S. (2003), Public-key support for group collaboration, *ACM Transactions on Information and System Security (TISSEC)*, Vol. 6, No. 4, pp. 547 – 565.

Ford, B., Strauss, J., Lesniewski-Laas, C., Rhea, S., Kaashoeck, F., and Morris, R. (2006), "Persistent personal names for globally connected mobile devices", *Proceedings of the 7th USENIX Symposium on Operating Systems Design and Implementation (OSDI)*.

Hsiao, H.-C., Lin, Y.-H., Studer, A., Studer, C., Wang, K.-H., Kikuchi, H., Perrig, A., Sun, H.-M., and Yang, B.-Y. "A study of user-friendly hash comparison schemes", *Proceedings of the 2009 Annual Computer Security Applications Conference, ACSAC '09*, Washington DC, USA, 2009, pp. 105 - 114.

Josefsson, S. (2006), *The Base16, Base32, and Base64 Data Encodings, RFC4648*, https://tools.ietf.org/html/rfc4648 (Accessed 28 March 2013)

Karayumak, F., Kauer, M., Olembo, M. M., Volk, T., & Volkamer, M. (2011), "User study of the improved Helios voting system interfaces", *2011 1st Workshop on Socio-Technical Aspects in Security and Trust (STAST)*, pp. 37 - 44).

Lin, Y.-H., Studer, A., Hsiao, H.-C., McCune, J. M., Wang, K.-H., Krohn, M., Lin, P.-L., Perrig, A., Sun, H.-M., and Yang, B.-Y. (2009), "Spate: Small-group PKI-less Authenticated Trust Establishment", *Proceedings of the 7th International Conference on Mobile Systems, Applications and Services*, pp. 1 – 14.

Perrig, A., and Song, D. (1999), "Hash visualization: A new technique to improve real-world security", *Proceedings of the 1999 International Workshop on Cryptographic Techniques and E-Commerce*, pp. 131 - 138.

Reynolds, R. E., White, R. M., and Hilgendorf, R. L. (1972), "Detection and recognition of colored signal lights", *Human Factors* Vol. 14, No. 3, pp. 227 - 236.

Shepard, R. N. (1967), "Recognition memory for words, sentences and pictures", *Journal of Verbal Learnings and Verbal Behaviour*, Vol. 6, Issue 1, pp. 156 - 163.

Chapter 2

Digital Forensics & Incident Analysis

Visual Triage of Email Network Narratives for Digital Investigations

J. Haggerty[1], S. Haggerty[2] and M.J. Taylor[3]

[1]School of Computing, Science & Engineering, University of Salford, Greater Manchester, M5 4WT
[2]School of Humanities, University of Nottingham, Nottingham, NG7 2RD
[3]School of Computing & Mathematical Sciences, Liverpool John Moores University, Liverpool, L3 3AF
e-mail : J.Haggerty@salford.ac.uk; sheryllynne.haggerty@nottingham.ac.uk; M.J.Taylor@ljmu.ac.uk

Abstract

Email remains a key source of evidence during a digital investigation. The forensics examiner may be required to triage and analyse large email data sets for evidence. Current practice utilises tools and techniques that require a manual trawl through such data, which is a time-consuming process. Recent research has focused on speeding up analysis through the use of data visualization and the quantitative analysis of emails, for example, by analysing actor relationships identified through this medium. However, these approaches are unable to analyse the qualitative content, or narrative, of the emails themselves to provide a much richer picture of the evidence. This paper posits a novel approach which combines both quantitative and qualitative analysis of emails using data visualization to elucidate qualitative information for the forensics examiner. In this way, the examiner is able to triage large volumes of emails to identify actor relationships as well as their network narrative. In order to demonstrate the applicability of this methodology, this paper applies it to a case study of email data.

Keywords

Digital forensics, email, social networks, narrative, data visualization

1. Introduction

With the rapid development of technological applications, users are sophisticated consumers and increasingly demand larger data storage. This large amount of data adds complexity to a digital investigation because it must be triaged and searched for evidence relevant to the case. For example, in one investigation, police officers analysed 100,000 indecent images of children and 10,000 emails for the prosecution of a paedophile ring involving four individuals (BBC, 2012). This is extremely time consuming because current practice utilises tools and techniques that require manual analysis of email files.

Email data differs from other file types in that it may elucidate quantitative and qualitative information to the forensics examiner. Recent research in this area has focused on the quantitative analysis of emails, for example, by analysing actor relationships identified through this medium. However, these approaches are unable to analyse the qualitative content, or narrative, of the emails themselves to provide a much richer picture of the evidence. This paper therefore posits TagSNet, a novel approach which combines both quantitative and qualitative analysis of emails using data visualization. As will be demonstrated by the case study, the examiner is able to triage large volumes of emails to identify actor relationships as well as their network narrative. In this way, they will be able to prioritize their search for potential evidence relevant to the investigation.

This paper is organised as follows. Section 2 discusses related work. Section 3 posits TagSNet for the triage of quantitative and qualitative email data. Section 4 presents the results of applying the methodology to a case study. Finally, we make our conclusions in section 5 and discuss further work.

2. Related work

Due to the complexity and volume of data available today, there is much interest in data visualization of narratives outside the digital forensics domain. For example, Segel & Heer (2010) and Hullman & Diakopoulos (2011) propose visualization approaches using data produced by media organisations for conveying rhetoric, for example, political discussions in news stories. These approaches posit design strategies for visualization and interpretation of narratives. Fisher et al (2008) posit *Narratives*, an approach to visualize key words over time. This approach visualizes a sequence(s) of key words as a series of related line graphs. They suggest that this approach could be used for tracking items or actors of interest in news items and over time. Dou et al (2012) posit *LeadLine*, a tool to automatically detect events in news items and social media as well as support their exploration through visualization.

Other visualization approaches extend their analysis beyond Web data. For example, Nair et al (2011) posit how a patient's data may be better represented to clinicians by using documents to produce patient 'stories'. Wang et al (2011) posit a methodology for the analysis of large textual documents. This approach focuses on a central event and then analyses the relationship between this and other events. Ungar et al (2011) propose *IntentFinder*, a tool for the analysis and representation of data which attempts to link document and narrative information with a subject's social networks. What these approaches have in common is that they are not designed for forensics investigations, for example, by only allowing data to be mounted in read-only mode.

Commonly used computer forensic tools, such as Forensic Toolkit (FTK) (Access Data, 2013) and EnCase (Guidance Software, 2013) are used for the analysis of email clients on a suspect's computer. Whilst these tools provide a means for analysis of storage media, email data must be read manually. These applications provide a robust forensic analysis, however they are not designed to perform automated retrieval and analysis of potential qualitative evidence relating to social networks and email content. Moreover, they do not enable visualization of potentially large email data sets.

The advantages of using data visualization for large data sets have led to such approaches in digital forensics being posited. For example, Schrenk & Poisel (2011) discuss the requirements for visualization in digital investigations due to the volume of data that must be searched. Whilst they do not posit a single approach, they discuss methodologies for a range of visual exploration, such as time-related and email data. Osborne et al (2012) focus on visualizations to support the investigatory process rather than data to identify evidence *per se*. Jankun-Kelly et al (2009) posit an approach to investigate a range of documents, including Webcache files and email. This approach focuses on visualization of textual data rather than relationships between actors. Palomo et al (2011) focus on the visualization of network traffic through self-organising maps to identify anomalous behaviour or system intrusions. However, this approach focuses on the identification and visualization of network artefacts, such as source ports, destination addresses, protocols, etc. rather than social interactions between actors.

Other approaches to data visualization in digital forensics have focused on email as a potential source of evidence. For example, Haggerty et al (2011) use the Enron email corpus as a case study to propose a method for the triage and analysis of actors within an email network. Henseler (2010), who also uses the Enron data set, suggests an approach for filtering large email collections during an investigation based on statistical and visualisation techniques. Wiil et al (2010) provide an analysis of the 9/11 hijackers' network and focus on the relationships between these actors. This study uses a number of measures associated with social network analysis to identify key nodes. However, these approaches only focus on the quantitative analysis of actor relationships rather than the qualitative information within the emails themselves. There is therefore a requirement for combining both quantitative and qualitative data during an investigation to not only visualize the actors involved, but also to analyse what is being discussed, i.e. the network narrative.

3. Overview of TagSNet

As suggested in sections 1 and 2, the key challenges to computer forensics email investigations are: the volume of data, evidence identification, relevant social network identification and visual representation of evidence. This section posits the TagSNet tool for visualization of quantitative and qualitative email data to meet these challenges and triage evidence.

Currently, there is no accepted definition of the term 'network narrative'. In related literature, a network comprises a set of actors and the relations between them and the network itself. A narrative is the discourse in relation to network events or effects. We therefore define 'network narrative' as the discourse with regard to a set of actors, their relationships and events pertaining to them. Identifying the network narrative allows us to assess the impact of endogenous and exogenous events of interest on the network(s) and content discovered during an investigation.

In order to analyse the network narrative in this context, the authors have developed TagSNet (**Tag** cloud and **S**ocial **Net**works), to visualise the quantitative and qualitative data in emails. This software extends the *Matrixify* (Haggerty & Haggerty, 2011) temporal social network analysis tool. Actor relationship information is conveyed through social network diagrams and the content of the emails through TagSNet. These visualisations are not aimed at answering questions *per se*, but to enable a forensics examiner to triage email data more quickly than a manual trawl.

As discussed above, emails contain both quantitative and qualitative data. The quantitative data in emails refers to the social networks that they may elucidate. A social network is an interconnected group or system and the relations, both logical and physical, between the actors. There is a tendency to assume that just because actors are linked they must form a cohesive and positive social network. However, this is not necessarily the case and the relationships between network members must be explored to fully understand how these networks function (Haggerty et al, 2011). The network views in TagSNet are ego-centric in nature due to the source material, i.e. we do not know the relationships between actors beyond those identified in the suspect's emails. The qualitative data refers to the content of the emails. Rather than reading individual emails to build up a picture of the discussions and themes in the network narrative, TagSNet identifies and quantifies the qualitative data. Through this data mining, key words are identified as they re-occur, thereby identifying the network narrative concerns.

These two elements combined provide a rich picture of the network events and relationships over time, including reactions to endogenous and exogenous events. Of interest to the forensics examiner are the following:

- Key actors
- Actor relationships in the network at specific times
- Key narratives in the network
- Change over time (e.g. pre- and post-criminal activity)
- The identification of further evidence sources or lines of enquiry in either quantitative or qualitative data

As with any investigation, the data must be acquired in a robust manner, ensuring that the evidence maintains its integrity. Therefore, emails are imported into TagSNet in read-only mode to avoid data modification. These email files are located in client-specific directories. For example, Mozilla Thunderbird stores email data in text format in mbox files under the following directories dependent on the operating system: C:\Documents and Settings\[UserName]\ApplicationData\Thunderbird\ Profiles\ (Windows XP), ~/.thunderbird/xxxxxxxx.default/ (Linux) and ~/Library/Thunderbird/Profiles/ xxxxxxxx.default/ (Mac OS X) (Haggerty et al, 2011).

As illustrated in figure 1, the software has, at its most basic level, three main areas of functionality; file reading and processing (data mining), visualization, and graphical output. These functional points are covered in more detail below.

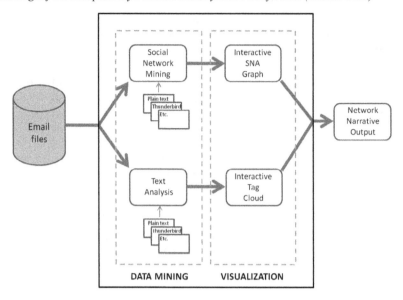

Figure 1: Overview of TagSNet

The email files are processed in two ways; for social network information and textual analysis. The social networks elucidated by the email files are derived from the FROM, TO, and CC data in both messages sent to and received by the suspect. This data includes the search of forwarded messages located under the main message. As noted above, this view of the network is a suspect-centric snapshot, i.e. as we are analyzing the suspect's computer, the social networks will be from the suspect's point of view. Textual analysis is achieved by creating a dictionary of all words in the email file and then counting their occurrence. These results are made available to the visualization function as the basis for text sizing. It is posited that the occurrence of words (or lack of) suggests their concern to the network. As such, commonly occurring words, such as 'the', 'a', 'to', etc. are ignored during this process. These words provide a useful function in language but their commonality adds noise to the visualizations without adding to the network narrative analysis. However, this function could be extended to include a user-defined dictionary of words to include or exclude in a search.

The results of this data mining are passed to the two visualization functions. A social network graph is constructed from the data passed from the social network mining function. This graph-building element visualises actors as network nodes, identifies the actors and produces lines to represent relationships between them. A tag cloud is created from the textual analysis results to produce the narrative view of qualitative data. This view sizes words in the email text by frequency of occurrence and these are placed using a random layout. Various sensitivity levels, or thresholds, can be applied to the data, based on popularity of words, to reduce noise, and highlight key concerns within the text. These visualizations together form output in the form of a network narrative. Both these visualizations are interactive in that the forensics examiner may move both actors and text around. This enhances the visualization by ensuring that the results can be explored and that the best layout can be chosen.

This section has provided an overview to the TagSNet approach for the analysis of network narratives in email data. In the next section, we demonstrate the applicability of the proposed approach for triaging evidence by applying it to email data from the Enron corpus.

4. Case study and results

Enron was a large energy company that employed thousands of workers across 40 countries. The Enron fraud resulted in the bankruptcy of the company and dissolution of a large accountancy and audit company. The main executives, such as the CEO Jeffrey Skilling, used a series of techniques to perpetrate the fraud, such as accountancy loopholes, employing special purpose entities and poor accountancy practices, in order to hide billions of dollars of debt that the company had accrued. The email corpus is available online at (EnronData.org, n.d.) and provides a useful test set for methodologies related to email data due to its size and complexity.

Three folders from the Skilling email account are used to illustrate the ability of TagSNet to triage data and prioritise searches. It should be noted that figures 2 to 4 demonstrate this triage process for the identification of potential evidence rather than to provide evidence of the fraud discussed above. Moreover, they do not provide measurements or layouts based on statistical measures of the network, such as centralities suggested in Haggerty et al (2011), as this is outside the scope of this paper. These email folders, Genie, Mark and Sent_Mail, are used for two reasons. First, they represent different aspects of Skilling's email use; a specific set of correspondence related to a business event, personal correspondence with a family member and general business email traffic. This allows us to compare narratives in different contexts. Second, ranging from a small (10 actors, 930 words and 6KB mbox file) to large (515 actors, 50,198 words and 299KB mbox file) data set evaluates the impact of data scaling on the approach.

Emails from the Enron corpus are converted to Thunderbird mbox format to aid data mining. As discussed in section 3, email header data is used to generate network diagrams whilst the text of the emails, i.e. content, is used to generate the tag clouds, combining to form the network narrative. The two views in TagSNet are shown in different windows. However, for aesthetic purposes and comparison, the frames have been removed to focus on the network narrative in this paper. Due to the size of the mbox files, different levels of sensitivity to content data mining have been used. For example, in small files, such as Genie, it is possible to show all keywords. However, in larger files, this creates background noise. Therefore, thresholds of word re-occurrence are used to reduce the amount of information that is returned in the visualization. TagSNet allows the user to set the threshold level to provide the best aesthetic view without distorting the evidence.

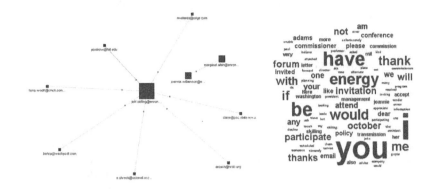

Figure 2: Genie folder network narrative

Figure 2 illustrates the Genie folder network narrative. This network comprises 10 emails, 10 actors and 930 words. Network nodes are sized by occurrence. All words are included in the visualization and the size of the font indicates their reoccurrence in the mbox file. The words highlighted in this view include; 'you', 'energy', 'invitation', 'participate', 'forum', 'October', 'attend', 'invited', 'policy', 'management', 'conference' and 'Washington'. Therefore, a qualitative analysis of the original emails suggests that this folder contains information that relates to the attendance at an energy forum in Washington organised by Skilling, and this is evident in the network narrative visualization.

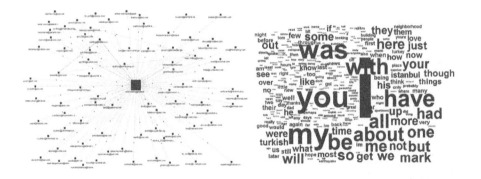

Figure 3: Mark folder network narrative

Figure 3 illustrates the Mark folder network narrative. This network comprises 55 emails, 84 actors and 28,064 words sent from a relative of Skilling. To reduce noise in the tag cloud, only words that occur more than ten times are included. The personal nature of the content is illustrated by the dominance of 'I' and 'my' in the network narrative view. In addition, other general but personal words, such as 'me', 'we', 'have', etc. dominate the view. However, within the network view, 'Istanbul' and 'Turkish' also appear. Therefore, a qualitative analysis of the original emails suggests that this a folder associated with personal messages from a family member, and there is some association with Turkey.

Figure 4: Sent_mail folder network narrative.

The Sent_Mail folder, as illustrated in figure 4, comprises 275 emails, 515 actors and 50,198 words. Again, to reduce noise, only words that occur more than 20 times are included in the tag cloud. This folder differs from the other two in that the content is far more general as they are emails related to Skilling's day-to-day business dealings. Two names are immediately apparent in the tag cloud, Jeff Skilling and Sherri Sera (Skilling's personal assistant) and this is supported by the network diagram. Indeed, many of the emails were sent by Sera on behalf of Skilling and were saved to this folder. This is illustrated by the prominence of her email address, 'sherrisera@enron.com' in the content as it appeared in the signature block. The use of words differs to those in the Mark folder in that they are obviously more related to business, for example, 'enron', 'fax', 'business', 'information', 'executive', 'company', 'assistant' and 'message'. Also highlighted is a location, 'Houston', where the business had its headquarters. Moreover, two numbers are also identified; '7136468381' and '7138535984'. These are the phone and fax numbers for Sera.

The three network narratives above quickly identify where to prioritise a manual trawl of emails for evidence using traditional forensic tools. In experiments, the average times to process and visualise the network narrative of the mbox files on a Windows 7 computer with a 2.5GHz Athlon Dual Core Processor and 4GB RAM were; Genie 0.5 secs, Mark 6.3 secs and Sent_Mail 9.4 secs. This is substantially quicker than manually reading the files to triage data. Given the personal nature of the Mark folder's emails, we may place this as a low priority unless the family member was somehow implicated in the case. We could also discount the Genie folder's emails, unless the case was related to the forum that took place in Washington. The highest priority would be the Sent_Mail folder for a number of reasons. First, it highlights the importance of Skilling's personal assistant in his business activities and would indicate that her email account may provide relevant evidence to the investigation. Second, as the emails are associated with business dealings, it may identify other actors of interest in the network views. Third, it highlights further potential sources of evidence, such as the phone numbers that are used, and therefore call logs, which could be beneficial to the investigator. It should be noted that in investigations involving emails, key words highlighted by the network narrative may be misleading as the actors involved may use codes. However, any unusual words would be highlighted in the visualizations and could be followed up in the manual analysis.

5. Conclusions and further work

Due to the amount of information email may provide to a forensics examiner, it remains a key source of evidence during a digital investigation. With our reliance on this medium, an examiner may be required to triage and analyse large email data sets. Current practice utilises tools and techniques that require a manual trawl through such data, which is a time-consuming process. Recent research has focused on data visualization to mitigate the effect of large data sets on an investigation. The approaches concerned with emails focus on the analysis of emails to identify social networks. However, these approaches are unable to analyse the qualitative, i.e. content (or narrative), of the emails themselves to provide a much richer picture of the evidence. This paper therefore posits a novel approach, TagSNet, which combines both quantitative (social networks) and qualitative (content) analysis of emails using data visualization that form the network narratives. As demonstrated by the case study, this approach can be used to triage data that may be of interest to the examiner to be followed up with manual searches for evidence specific to the case or to identify further sources of evidence. Further work aims to extend this approach to other media, such as online documents and social media.

6. References

Access Data (2013). http://www.accessdata.com. (Accessed 18 January 2013).

BBC (2012), http://www.bbc.co.uk/news/uk-england-19947914. (Accessed 18 January 2013).

Dou, W., Wang, X., Skau, D., Ribarsky, W. & Zhou, M.X (2012), "LeadLine: Interactive Visual Analysis of Text Data through Event Identification and Exploration", *Proceedings of the IEEE Symposium on Visual Analytics Science and Technology*, Seattle, USA, 2012, pp. 93-102.

EnronData.org (n.d.), http://enrondata.org/content/data/. (Accessed 18 January 2013).

Fisher, D., Hoff, A., Robertson, G. & Hurst, M. (2008), "Narratives: A Visualization to Track Narrative Events as they Develop", *Proceedings of the IEEE Symposium on Visual Analytics Science and Technology*, Columbus, USA, 2008, pp. 115-122.

Guidance Software (2013). http://www.guidancesoftware.com. (Accessed 18 January 2013).

Haggerty, J. and Haggerty, S. (2011), "Temporal Social Network Analysis for Historians: A Case Study", *Proceedings of the International Conference on Visualization Theory and Applications (IVAPP 2011)*, Algarve, Portugal, 2011, pp. 207 - 217.

Haggerty, J., Karran, A.J., Lamb, D.J. and Taylor, M.J. (2011), "A Framework for the Forensic Investigation of Unstructured Email Relationship Data", *International Journal of Digital Crime and Forensics*, Volume 3 Number 3, September 2011, pp. 1-18.

Henseler, H. (2010), "Network-based filtering for large email collections in E-Discovery", *Artificial Intelligence and Law*, Volume 18 Number 4, pp. 413-430.

Hullman, J. & Diakopoulos, N. (2011), "Visualization Rhetoric: Framing Effects in Narrative Visualization", *IEEE Transactions on Visualization and Computer Graphics*, Volume 17 Number 12, pp. 2231-2240.

Jankun-Kelly, T.J., Wilson, D., Stamps, A.S., Franck, J., Carver, J. & Swan II, J.E. (2009), "A Visual Analytic Framework for Exploring Relationships in Textual Contents of Digital Forensics Evidence", *Proceedings of the 6th International Workshop on Visualization for Cyber Security*, Atlantic City, USA, 2009, pp. 39-44.

Nair, V., Kaduskar, M., Bhaskaran, P., Bhaumik, S. & Lee, H. (2011), "Preserving Narratives in Electronic Health Records", *Proceedings of the International Conference on Bioinformatics and Biomedicine*, Atlanta, USA, 2011, pp. 418-421.

Palomo, E.J., North, J., Elizondo, D., Luque, R.M. & Watson, T. (2011), "Visualization of Network Forensics Traffic Data with Self-Organizing Map for Qualitative Features", *Proceedings of the International Joint Conference on Neural Networks*, San Jose, USA, 2011, pp. 1740-1747.

Schrenk, G. & Poisel, R. (2011), "A Discussion of Visualization Techniques for the Analysis of Digital Evidence", *Proceedings of the 6th International Conference on Availability, Reliability and Security*, Vienna, Austria, 2011, pp. 758-763.

Osborne, G., Turnbull, B. & Slay, J. (2012), "Development of InfoVis Software for Digital Forensics", *Proceedings of the 36th International Conference on Software and Applications Workshop*, Izmir, Turkey, 2012, pp. 213-217.

Segel, E. & Heer, J. (2010), "Narrative Visualization: Telling Stories with Data", *IEEE Transactions on Visualization and Computer Graphics*, Volume 16 Number 6, pp. 1139-1148.

Ungar, L., Leibholz, S. & Chaski, C. (2011), "IntentFinder: A System for Discovering Significant Information Implicit in Large, Heterogeneous Document Collections", *Proceedings of the International Conference on Technologies for Homeland Security*, Waltham, USA, 2011, pp. 219-223.

Wang, D., Liu, W., Xu, W. & Zhang, X. (2011), "Topic Tracking Based on Event Network", *Proceedings of the International Conferences on Internet of Things, and Cyber, Physical and Social Computing*, Dalian, China, 2011, pp. 488-493.

Wiil, U.K., Gniadek, J. & Memon, N. (2010), "Measuring Link Importance in Terrorist Networks", *Proceedings of the International Conference on Social Networks Analysis and Mining*, Odense, Denmark, 2010, pp. 225-232.

An Ontological Framework for a Cloud Forensic Environment

N.M. Karie[1,2], H.S. Venter[1]

[1]Department of Computer Science, University of Pretoria, Private Bag X20, Hatfield 0028, Pretoria, South Africa
[2]Department of Computer Science, Kabarak University, Private Bag - 20157, Kabarak, Kenya
E-mail: menza06@hotmail.com, hventer@cs.up.ac.za

Abstract

Cloud computing is an emerging field and is considered to be one of the most transformative technologies in the history of computing. This is so because it is radically changing the way how information technology services are created, delivered, accessed and managed. Cloud forensics, on the other hand, is utilising network forensics – a subset of digital forensic techniques – in a cloud environment. However, with the continued evolution from internet-based applications to cloud computing, the environments and components surrounding cloud forensics can easily become incomprehensible. In this paper, therefore, we present an ontological framework meant to provide a structure and depiction of the different cloud environments and components an investigator should be acquainted with, in the case of a cloud investigation process. In addition, we show the relationships and interactions between the different environments by capturing their content and boundaries. Furthermore, the purpose of this paper is meant to provide a common ontological framework for sharing coherent cloud computing concepts and also promote the understanding of the cloud environments and cloud components. Finally, the ontological framework presents an approach towards structuring and organizing the environments and components surrounding the cloud and constitutes the main contribution of this paper.

Keywords

Cloud forensics, cloud computing, cloud environments, cloud components, ontological framework

1. Introduction

With the emergence of cloud computing technologies, the need for cloud forensics has become inevitable. This is due to the notion of cloud computing opening a whole new world of possibilities for criminals to exploit. This also means that criminals can now use cloud computing environments to share information and to reinforce their hacking techniques (Garfinkel, 2011). As a result, the major potential security risks, such as malicious insiders, data loss/leakage and policy violations now invade the existing cloud environments.

Cloud forensics, as defined by Ruan et al (2011), is an emerging field that deals with the application of digital forensic techniques in cloud computing environments and forms a subset of network forensics. Technically, cloud forensics follows most of the main phases of network forensic processes. The only difference is that such phases are simply extended with techniques tailored for cloud computing environments within each phase. However, the continued widespread deployment of the Internet-based applications and network-enabled devices in an effort to support mechanisms for cloud computing, can potentially render the cloud environments and components incomprehensible.

In this paper we present an ontological framework in an attempt to provide a structure and depiction of the different cloud environments (cloud deployment models) and cloud components (cloud service models) that an investigator should be well-versed with in the case of an investigation processes involving the cloud. In addition, the proposed framework also shows the relationships and interactions between the different cloud environments and the cloud components. Furthermore, this paper provides a novel contribution and offers a simplified ontological framework that can, for example, help investigators comprehend the cloud environment and components with less effort.

As for the remaining part of this paper, section 2 presents previous and related work while section 3 briefly explains the cloud environments and components. The proposed ontological framework is presented in section 4 followed by a discussion in section 5. Finally, section 6 presents the conclusion and future work.

2. Related Work

There exist several frameworks in cloud computing proposed by other researchers, which have made valuable contributions towards the development of the ontological framework presented in this paper. In this section, therefore, a summary of some of the most prominent efforts in previous research work is provided.

To begin with, Hoefer and Karagiannis (2010) argues that several organisations want to explore the possibilities and benefits of cloud computing. However, with the amount of cloud computing services increasing quickly, the need for taxonomy frameworks rises. In their paper they describe the available cloud computing services and propose a tree-structured taxonomy based on their characteristics, in order to easily classify cloud computing services so that it is easier to compare them. However, in this paper, we focus on an ontological framework meant to provide a common framework to share coherent cloud computing concepts as well as to promote the understanding of cloud environments and essential cloud components. Such a framework will assist investigators, for example, in planning of investigation techniques to be employed in specific cloud environments in the case of an investigation process and thus enhancing the investigation of criminal cases involving the cloud.

Yan (2011) argues that cloud computing, as a service, provides a luring environment for criminals and increases the difficulties of digital forensics. He then presents a forensic framework that focuses on the security issues of cloud services in order to beat cybercrime. Yan's framework, however, focuses on security issues of cloud services while we, in the current proposed ontological framework, focus on structuring and organising the different cloud environments and cloud components.

In their paper, Takahashi et al (2010) propose an ontological approach to cybersecurity in cloud computing. They built an ontology for cybersecurity operational information based on actual cybersecurity operations mainly focused on non-cloud computing. In order to discuss necessary cybersecurity information in cloud computing, they apply the ontology to cloud computing. Their work is centred on cybersecurity operations. However, the current framework is centred on, as mentioned earlier, cloud environments and cloud components.

Lamia et al (2009) also explains that the progress of research efforts in a novel technology is contingent on having a rigorous organisation of its knowledge domain and a comprehensive understanding of all the relevant components and their relationships of the technology. In their paper, they propose an ontology for cloud computing which demonstrates a dissection of the cloud into five main layers. However, there work does not elaborate on the cloud environments and cloud components in the way that is presented in this paper.

There also exist other related works on ontological frameworks, but neither those nor the cited references in this paper have presented an ontological framework for the cloud environments and cloud components in the way that is introduced in this paper. However, we acknowledge the fact that the previous proposed frameworks have offered useful insights toward the development of the ontological framework in this paper. In the section that follows we briefly explain the different cloud environments and components based on our review of the literature.

3. Cloud Environments and cloud Components

Cloud Computing is an emerging technology that uses the internet and remotely located servers to maintain data and applications. The 'cloud', therefore, can be viewed as a network of virtual machines geographically dispersed. Cloud computing technology is creating a revolution in computer architecture, software and tools development. Furthermore, it is changing the way organizations store, distribute and consume information. In this section of the paper, the authors explain the different cloud environments and cloud components that form the basis of the proposed ontological framework.

3.1. The Cloud Environments (Cloud Deployment Models)

3.1.1. Public Cloud Environment

A public cloud is one in which a service provider makes resources, such as applications, platforms and infrastructures available to the general public over the internet. Public clouds are owned and operated at datacentres belonging to the service providers and are shared by multiple customers (Subramanian, 2011a). This also means that, public clouds offer unlimited storage space and increased bandwidth via internet to any organisation across the globe. Such services on the public cloud may be offered free or on a pay-per-usage model. The degree of visibility and control of public clouds depends on the delivery mode. However, there is less visibility and control in public clouds compared to private clouds because the underlying infrastructure is owned by the service providers.

3.1.2. Private Cloud Environment

A private cloud can be viewed as the implementation of cloud computing services on resources dedicated to an organisation (i.e. the organisation owns the hardware and software), whether they exist on-premises or off-premises. A private cloud gives an organisation the advantage of greater control over the entire stack, from the bare metal up to the services accessible to users (Ubuntu, 2013).

3.1.3. Community Cloud Environment

A Community cloud is one that is tailored to the shared needs of a business community. Community clouds are operated specifically for a targeted group. Usually, such groups (communities) have similar cloud requirements and their ultimate goal is to work together to achieve their business objectives. According to Techopedia (2013), community clouds are often designed for businesses and organisations working on joint projects, applications, or research, which requires a central cloud computing facility for building, managing and executing such projects, regardless of the solution rented. The infrastructure in a community cloud is shared by several organizations with common concerns such as (security, compliance, jurisdiction, etc.), whether managed internally or by a third-party or hosted internally or externally. The cost is, however, shared by all the participating organizations.

3.1.4. Hybrid Cloud Environment

A hybrid cloud is a combination of both public and private clouds (Subramanian, 2011b). This means that a vendor who owns a private cloud can form a partnership with a public cloud provider, or a public cloud provider can form a partnership with a vendor that provides private cloud platforms. However, according to Mell and Grance (2011) of the National Institute of Standards and Technology (NIST), a hybrid cloud is a composition of two or more public, private, or community cloud infrastructures that remain unique entities but are bound together by either standardised or proprietary technology that enables data and application portability. Using the hybrid cloud architecture, organisations and individuals are able to obtain degrees of fault tolerance combined with locally immediate usability without dependency on internet connectivity. This is due to some of the resources in a hybrid cloud being managed in-house while others are provided externally. In the next sub-section the authors elaborate on the essential cloud components which also form part of the proposed ontological framework in this paper.

3.2. The Essential Cloud Components (Cloud Service Models)

Whichever the cloud environment deployed, cloud service providers will always offer their clients (individuals and organisations) with the following three categories of cloud service models: Infrastructure-as-a-Service (IaaS), Platform-as-a-Service

(PaaS) and Software-as-a-Service (SaaS). In the next sub-sections, these service models are further explained.

3.2.1. Infrastructure-as-a-Service (IaaS)

IaaS is a cloud computing service model that offers physical and virtual systems (cloud computing infrastructure), including an operating system, hypervisor, raw storage, and networks (Oracle Corporation, 2012). Servers represent the main computing resource in IaaS and are often virtual instances within a physical server. The service providers usually own the computing infrastructure and are responsible for housing, running and maintaining it. On the other hand, organisations pay on a per-use basis. IaaS helps organisations realize cost savings and efficiencies while modernising and expanding their information technology capabilities without spending capital resources on infrastructure (GAS, 2013).

3.2.2. Platform-as-a-Service (PaaS)

PaaS as explained in an expert group report by the European Commission (2010) provides computational resources (cloud computing platforms) via a platform upon which applications and services can be developed and hosted. PaaS typically makes use of dedicated APIs to control the behaviour of a server hosting engine which executes and replicates the execution according to user requests. Cloud computing platforms may include the operating system, the programming language execution environment, the database, and the web server. PaaS also allows clients to use the virtualised servers and associated services for running applications or developing and testing new applications.

3.2.3. Software-as-a-Service (SaaS)

SaaS sometimes referred to as Service or Application Clouds (European Commission, 2010) offers implementations of specific business functions and business processes that are provided with specific cloud capabilities. I.e. they provide cloud computing applications or services using a cloud infrastructure or platform, rather than providing cloud features themselves. Moreover, SaaS also provides internet-based access to different software, thus presenting new opportunities for software vendors to explore. In the next section, the proposed ontological framework is presented and explained.

4. The Proposed Ontological Framework

In this section of the paper the authors present the proposed ontological framework. Figure 1 shows the structure of the ontological framework. Note that, due to the small font size of Figure 1, Figures 2 to 4 contains enlarged extracts of the ontological framework as depicted in Figure 1.

The framework consists of five layers arranged from left to right and with the first layer depicting the main domain of focus (i.e. the cloud/cloud computing). This is followed by the cloud environments in the second layer and the essential cloud components in the third layer. Services and service providers are introduced in the fourth and fifth layer of the ontological framework as a way of representing individual, finer-grained details of the essential cloud components, also referred to as cloud service models.

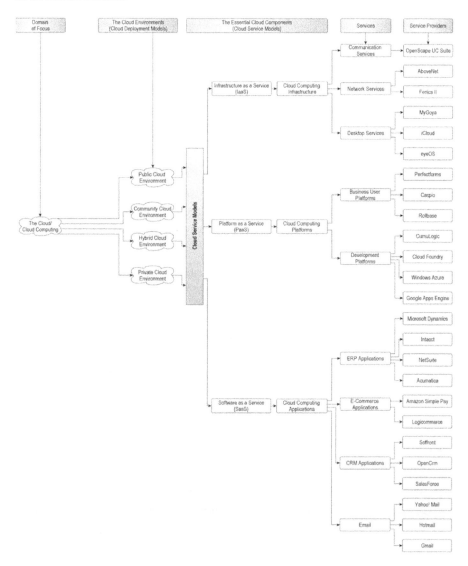

Figure 1: Conceptualisation of the cloud environments and essential components

Cloud service models enable software, platform and infrastructure to be delivered as services. The term service is used to reflect the fact that they are provided on demand and are paid for, on a usage basis (Czarnecki, 2011). In the authors' experience, organising the framework into the particular cloud environments, essential cloud components, services and service providers, was necessary to simplify the

117

understanding of the framework as well as to present specific finer details of the framework. The services and service providers listed in the fourth and fifth layers (see Figure 1) were only selected as common examples to facilitate this study and should not be treated as an exhaustive list.

The major areas explored (with their details as shown in Figure I) include the cloud environments, the essential cloud components, services and the service providers. For the purpose of this study, the cloud environments (cloud deployment models) are divided into public cloud environment, private cloud environment, community cloud environment and hybrid cloud environment. The essential cloud components (cloud service models), on the other hand, are divided into Infrastructure-as-a-Service (IaaS), Platform-as-a-Service (PaaS) and Software-as-a-Service (SaaS). However, infer from Figure 1 that the IaaS, PaaS and SaaS are accessible through cloud computing infrastructure, cloud computing platforms and cloud computing applications respectively.

The cloud computing infrastructure (see Figure 2) is further divided into communication services, network services and desktop services forming the fourth layer of the ontological framework. The communication services show OpenScape UC Suite as one of the service providers. The network services have AboveNet™ and Fenics II as service providers. Finally, desktop services show MyGoya, iCloud and eyeOS as service providers. The service providers form the fifth layer of the framework as shown in Figure 1. However, note that, the contents of the fourth and fifth layer (services and service providers) in Figure1 were introduced in this framework to provide only selected examples for the purpose of this study. Therefore, such contents should not be treated as an exhaustive list.

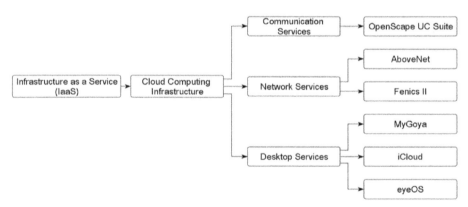

Figure 2: Infrastructure-as-a-Service

The cloud computing platforms as shown in Figure 3 are divided into two: business user platforms and development platforms. Business user platforms have PerfectForms, Caspio™ and Rollbase as service providers. The development platforms show CumuLogic, Cloud Foundry™, Windows Azure™, and Google™ Apps Engine as selected service providers. However as said earlier these are only common examples for the purpose of this study and should not be treated as an exhaustive list.

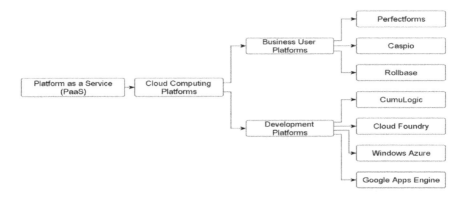

Figure 3: Platform-as-a-Service

The cloud computing applications shown in Figure 4 are divided into Enterprise Resource Planning (ERP) applications, E-commerce applications, Customer Relationship Management (CRM) applications and Email as selected examples. The ERP applications have Microsoft Dynamics™, Intacct®, NetSuite and Acumatica as service providers. E-commerce applications show Amazon Simple Pay and Logicommerce™ as examples of service providers. The CRM applications have Soffront®, OpenCrm and SalesForce® as service providers. Finally, Email has Yahoo!®, Hotmail® and Gmail™ as examples of the service providers. As said earlier, these were only selected as common examples for the purpose of this framework and, therefore, should not be treated as an exhaustive list.

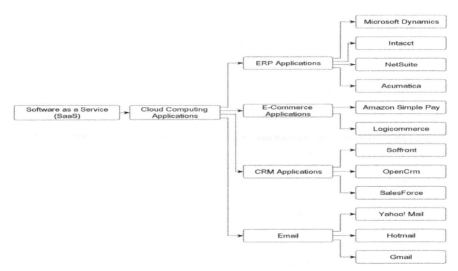

Figure 4: Software-as-a-Service

5. Discussion

The ontological framework presented in this paper is a new contribution and its scope is defined by the cloud environments, the essential cloud components, services and the service providers (see Figure 1). Such an ontological framework can be used, for example, as a common platform to share coherent cloud computing concepts and also promote the understanding of the cloud environments and cloud components. Moreover, the ontological framework can also serve, for example, as a basis for sharing common views of the structure and depiction of cloud computing information in a bid to enable the reuse of domain knowledge.

Furthermore, the framework in this paper can, for example, help investigators to explicitly describe investigation processes and procedures that focus on specific cloud environments in the case of cloud forensics. In addition, forensic tools developers can also use the ontological framework to fine-tune their tools so as to be able to cover as many potential security risks and policy violations experienced in the different cloud environments. This also implies that developers will find the ontological framework in this paper constructive, especially when considering new cloud forensic techniques for specific cloud environments.

In the case of cloud forensics, the proposed ontological framework can also assist in the design and development of high-tech acquisition tools incorporating, for example, hybrid cloud architectural designs with shareable features such as automated acquisition, reporting, visualisation and presentation of evidence in a manner that is acceptable in a court of law. Moreover, such high-tech tools will also enhance the investigation of criminal cases involving multiple cloud computing environments.

The proposed ontological framework can also be useful, for example, in cloud interoperability and exchanging of information between the different cloud environments. Moreover, it can be helpful in the design and development of standardised technology that also enables data and application portability in the different cloud environments. This is backed up by the fact that, the framework has explicitly described the distinctions of the various cloud environments, essential cloud components, services and service providers shown in Figure 1.

Finally, the ontological framework is, therefore, a new contribution towards advancing the field of cloud computing. To the best of the authors' knowledge, there exists no other work of this kind and, therefore, this is a novel contribution towards advancing the cloud computing and cloud forensic domain.

6. Conclusion and Future Work

The problem addressed in this paper was that of the incomprehensible cloud environments and components we are currently faced with. This incomprehensibility has been caused by the continued evolution from internet-based applications to cloud computing. In this paper we have proposed an ontological framework that provides a structure and a depiction of the different cloud environments and cloud components as a way to help individuals comprehend them with less effort. In addition, the cloud environments, the essential cloud components, services and service providers were also captured in the framework and explained. Therefore, the authors believe that by using this ontological framework a better understanding of the cloud environments and associated cloud components can be gained. However, more research needs to be conducted in order to identify new components and also to improve on the proposed ontological framework in this paper. Finally, the framework should spark further discussion on the development of new cloud computing ontological frameworks.

7. References

Czarnecki, C., (2011), "Cloud Service Models: Comparing SaaS PaaS and IaaS", *Perspectives on Cloud Computing & Training from Learning Tree International.* Available at: http://cloud-computing.learningtree.com/2011/11/09/cloud-service-models-comparing-saas-paas-and-iaas/ [Accessed February 13, 2013].

European Commission, (2010), Editors: Jeffery, K. and Neidecker-Lutz, B., "The future of cloud computing", opportunities for European cloud computing beyond 2010. *Expert Group Report*

GAS, (2013), Infrastructure as a Service (IaaS). Available at: http://www.gsa.gov/portal/content/112063 [Accessed March 20, 2013].

Garfinkel, S.L., (2011), The Criminal Cloud, *MIT Technology Review*, Available at: http://www.technologyreview.com/news/425770/the-criminal-cloud/ [Accessed February 4, 2013].

Hoefer, C.N., Karagiannis, G., (2010), "Taxonomy of cloud computing services", *Proceedings of the GLOBECOM Workshops*, pp.1345-1350

Lamia, Y., Butrico, M., and Da Silva, D., (2008), "Toward a Unified Ontology of Cloud Computing", *Proceedings of the Grid Computing Environments Workshop*, pp.1-10

Mell, P. and Grance, T., (2011), "The NIST Definition of cloud computing", *Recommendations of the National Institute of Standards and Technology.*

Oracle Corporation, (2012), "Making Infrastructure-as-a-Service in the Enterprise a Reality", *An Oracle White Paper.*

Ruan, K., Carthy, J., Kechadi, T. and Crosbie, M., (2011), "Cloud forensics", *Proceedings of the 7th IFIP WG 11.9 International Conference on Digital Forensics 2011*, Orlando, FL, USA

Subramanian, K., (2011a), "Public Clouds", *A whitepaper sponsored by Trend Micro Inc.*

Subramanian, K., (2011b), "Hybrid Clouds", *A whitepaper sponsored by Trend Micro Inc.*

Takahashi, T., Kadobayashi, Y. and Fujiwara, H., (2010) "Ontological Approach toward Cybersecurity in Cloud Computing", *Proceedings of the 3rd international conference on Security of information and networks (SIN '10), ACM, New York, NY, USA*, pp 100-109

Techopedia, (2013), "Community Cloud", Available at: http://www.techopedia.com/definition/26559/community-cloud [Accessed February 8, 2013]

Ubuntu, (2013), "Private cloud", Available at: http://www.ubuntu.com/cloud/private-cloud [Accessed February 8, 2013].

Yan, C., (2011), "Cybercrime Forensic System in Cloud Computing", *Proceedings of the Image Analysis and Signal Processing (IASP) Conference*, pp.612-615

MetaFor: Metadata Signatures for Automated Remote File Identification in Forensic Investigations

M.P. Roberts and J. Haggerty

School of Computing, Science & Engineering, University of Salford, Greater Manchester, M5 4WT

matt.concordia@gmail.com; J.Haggerty@salford.ac.uk

Abstract

The increased use of the Internet to store data ensures that it provides a valuable resource for a forensics examiner during an investigation. Of particular interest is evidence related to the dissemination of indecent images of children that are spread via social networking sites and Web fora. This paper posits a novel approach, MetaFor, which using a Web crawler searches for metadata signatures for automated identification of files residing on remote Web servers. In this way, it may identify potential repositories of illegal images or sources of evidence related to traditional crimes, such as utilising geo-location metadata to identify digital pictures taken during a crime in progress. This approach differs from other forensic signature schemes in that it utilises JPEG header metadata rather than image or file data as the basis of a signature. In this way, MetaFor can be extended to search for unknown files that may be relevant to an investigation. In order to demonstrate the applicability of the approach, this paper applies the approach to a case study of two Web servers and presents the results.

Keywords

Digital forensics, signature analysis, image files

1. Introduction

Today's reliance on technology has brought many economic and cultural benefits, but it also harbours many technical and social challenges. One major benefit of this wide scale adoption of technology is the speed and volume of data and information that may be shared amongst hosts. However, this has given rise to concerns over paedophile activity and the spread of illegal digital pictures, in particular indecent images of children, via social networking sites and Web fora (see for example, BBC, 2012).

Owing to the number and prolific nature of the media files themselves, forensic examiners have a hard, and at times disturbing, duty to find and identify indecent images of children disseminated online. Limited time and budgets make thorough manual searching unrealistic or at best, a time-consuming and costly process due to the amount of data that must be searched. Moreover, most image identification techniques involve computationally expensive algorithms in order to assess image data resident in a file in an attempt to evade anti-forensics techniques employed by a suspect. This paper presents a novel application, MetaFor, by which a forensics examiner may run an automated Web crawler search of Web servers for known suspicious or illegal images by utilising signatures formed from JPEG metadata. In this way, it may automatically identify potential repositories of illegal images or sources of evidence related to traditional crimes, such as utilising geo-location metadata to identify digital pictures taken during a crime in progress. As will be discussed in section 3, this approach has the added functionality of extending the search to unknown images residing online.

This paper is organised as follows. Section 2 discusses related work. Section 3 presents an overview of the system and describes the signature scheme. Section 4 presents the results of applying the approach to a case study. Finally, we make our conclusions in section 5 and discuss further work.

2.   Related work

Commonly used computer forensic tools, such as Forensic Toolkit (FTK) (Access Data, 2013) and EnCase (Guidance Software, 2013) are used for storage media analysis of a variety of files and data types in fully integrated environments. For example, FTK can perform tasks such as file extraction, make a forensic image of data on storage media, recover deleted files, determine data types and text extraction. EnCase is widely used within law enforcement and like FTK provides a powerful interface to the hard drive or data source under inspection, for example, by providing a file manager that shows extant and deleted files. Whilst these applications provide a robust forensic analysis, they are not designed to perform automated retrieval and analysis of potential evidence residing on remote Web servers.

Due to the volume of potential evidence that may require analysis, there is a requirement for automated approaches for file identification. The tools above enable searches of file hashes. However, due to the vulnerability of this approach to anti-forensics techniques, other signature schemes have been proposed. For example, FORSIGS (Haggerty & Taylor, 2007) searches for sixteen random bytes located in a single memory location which forms the file signature. This has been extended to online searches in FORWEB (Haggerty et al, 2008) which employs a Web spider to crawl through a web page to collect links to image files. These images are then downloaded and assessed using the FORSIGS algorithm. Alternatively, Mohamad & Deris (2009) use a single-byte marker and a twenty-point reference for signature detection. These signature approaches can also be extended to search within slack space on the storage media (Holleboom & Garcia, 2011).

Content-based image retrieval (CBIR) has been the subject of research for some time. CBIR is concerned with identifying an image file based on locating objects that are held within the image. Approaches, such as Sportiello & Zanero (2011), use a support vector machine (SVM) which is trained by human-directed input to recognise objects by grouping them based on attributes within the image file. These algorithms have had some success when applied to "stock" photos that are clean and usually uncluttered. Other schemes focus on identifying individual sources of digital images, such as cameras. For example, Chang-Tsun Li and Li (2012) propose a couple-decoupled photo response non-uniformity approach to improve the accuracy of device identification and for image content integrity verification. Kang et al (2012) propose a sensor pattern noise (SPN) approach for camera identification.

All of the above techniques analyse the image data or the whole of the file for their analysis. Alternative approaches propose the use of header information and in particular the EXIF data to identify files. For example, Kee et al (2011) posit that it would be possible to tell if the data held within the image header had been modified based on the fingerprint left by the make and model of the camera. This research created a 284-value signature taken from the EXIF data, thumbnail image, quantization values, and Huffman codes. Alternatively, Fan et al (2011) propose a scheme based on statistical analysis to detect image manipulation. However, these approaches have in common that they are not designed for forensic investigations, and in particular, the identification of images online.

3. MetaFor

This section provides an overview of the MetaFor approach. First, it describes the MetaFor architecture. In particular, it identifies the main features of the application. Second, it posits the signature scheme utilising metadata resident in JPEG image headers. Moreover, it describes how the scheme can be extended to search for unknown image files that may reside online that could provide further evidence to the forensics examiner. In this way, it may be used to automatically search for unknown online repositories of illegal images or digital pictures to support ongoing investigations.

A. System overview

The MetaFor architecture can be split into three main sections. First is the user interface to be used by the forensic examiner. Second is the signature management code that extracts, stores and manages the signatures to match against. Last is the search component itself. This part is responsible for searching a Web server for images and extracting any EXIF data for comparison with the signatures held locally. Figure 1 provides an overview of the system architecture.

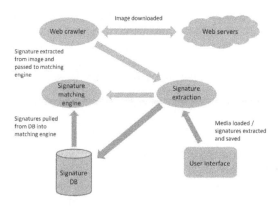

Figure 1: High level view of the system architecture

The user interface design is centred on a main page from which the configured search is initiated. Forms are used to add signatures, manage signature groups, configure the starting URLs and tune the application. The sub forms are all accessible via a menu system in the main window. The main window shows four progress bars each with two corresponding counters. These are present so that any component that is a bottleneck or that is used to a greater extent than others could be tuned by allocating more threads of this type. That is to say, if the signature extraction and comparison component queue is collecting work quicker than it can process then the ration of EXIF comparer threads can be increased to allocate more time to this process.

To enable an application to match a file against a signature, a permanent storage method needs to be established. In addition, the number of images of an illegal nature is always on the rise so there needs to be a mechanism to add more signatures and manage them appropriately. All of the permanent storage functionality is carried out "offline" in the sense that it can be separated, in temporal terms, from the main crawling and searching functionality. The database design is implemented in MySQL. The structure mirrors the abstraction of a signature being made up from many signature segments, where a segment is representative of an EXIF tag and its value. Signatures belong to a parent Signature Group which allows grouping of signatures for reporting or administrative purposes.

The search functionality is separated into four main components. The HTML Downloader component is responsible for sending an HTTP request to the Web server and receiving the response. The HTML Parser searches through the HTML and pulls out paths to images and links to other Web pages if the depth is set accordingly. The Image Downloader downloads part or the entire image found by the HTML Parser. Finally, the Signature Processor is the main work horse and is responsible for extracting the EXIF data from the downloaded image, converting it to a native format and then iterating through the signatures to see if any match.

B. Metadata signature scheme

Although JPEG is the commonly accepted term for the image format itself, the ITU-T Recommendation T.81 standard only covers the definition of the codec. This defines how to compress a stream of bytes (which in this case is data that represents an image) and how to decompress them back again, in order to view the image. There are four modes that the standard defines, namely: sequential Discrete Cosine Transformation (DCT) based, progressive DCT based, lossless, and hierarchical (ITU, 1992). The predominant method used over the Internet is the sequential DCT based technique.

The file format that is used to structure the JPEG compressed data is commonly the JPEG File Interchange Format (JFIF). This format defines markers within the file to designate specific file sections and their lengths. The whole image is started by a start of image (SOI) marker designated by the hexadecimal value "FFD8" and ended by end of image (EOI) "FFD9". Other sections that are relevant are the compression data tables are held in sections DHT which holds one or more Huffman Tables. This is a process whereby commonly occurring byte patterns are replaced by a shorter "key". These key/value pairs are stored in the header in a Huffman Table for use when decoding. The DQT section which hold the quantization tables. Most pertinent are the application specific sections (APP*n*) designated by the hexadecimal marker "FFE*n*" where *n* is the number of the group. For example the EXIF application specific group is always defined as APP1 (FFE1 in hexadecimal). This signifies the start of the metadata which is used as the basis of a signature in our scheme.

The Exchangeable Image File Format (EXIF) was included in the Japan Electronic Industry Development Association Standard for Camera File System (DCF) (JEIDA, 1998). This standard describes how metadata is stored within an image or audio file header which can contain compressed or uncompressed data. The EXIF data is contained within the Application Marker Segment (APP1) section of the JPEG file. Following the APP1 marker and length the section is defined as EXIF data with the EXIF identifier code. Following this, the EXIF data is defined in a Tagged Image File Format (TIFF) structure. This structure is made up of multiple Image File Directories that contain specific data pertaining to a subject. For instance, IFD0 is the first Image File Directory (IFD) that holds the interoperability data. This is the data that describes (amongst others) the image data structure, the image data characteristics, picture-taking conditions and details such as the date and time it was taken. IFD1 contains data relevant to the thumbnail version of the image, including the image data itself. A further IFD will go on to describe Global Positioning Satellite (GPS) data that depicts where the picture was taken if the writing device is able to capture such data. Figure 1 depicts the structure as per the 1998 JEIDA standard.

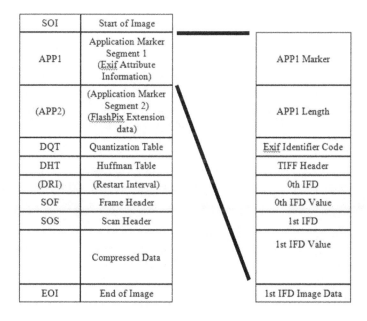

Figure 1: JEIDA EXIF data structure

Data inside each IFD are depicted by structures called tags. Tags translate to an EXIF field, ultimately describing a field/value pair. These tags are identified by a unique 2-byte number to identify the field. The tag structure is made up from this identifier, a 2-byte type field that describes what data type the value pertaining to this field is, a 4-byte count that depicts how many values are included for this tag and a 4-byte offset value from the start of the TIFF header that points to the actual value for this tag. As an example the tag values describing the manufacturer of a camera held in IFD0 could look as follows and could form a metadata signature:

Bytes 0-1 (ID): 0x010f
Bytes 2-3 (Type): ASCII
Bytes 4-7 (Count): 1
Bytes 8-11 (Value Offset): 1
Byte 12-16 (Value): Canon

A metadata signature is added to a group in the Add Signature form in MetaFor in two ways. An image (or a directory full of images) can be selected and the signature(s) can be extracted from them and displayed on the form and saved to the database. Alternatively a signature can be compiled manually using logical expressions to allow a custom signature to describe a geographical area or a temporal range. For example, the following segments could be defined:

GPSLatitude : Less Than 51.861793
GPSLatitude: Greater Than 51.861731
GPSLongitude: Less Than -2.243199
GPSLongitude: More Than -2.243349
DateTimeOriginal: More Than 01 May 1973
DateTimeOriginal: Less Than 01 August 1979

This would return any pictures taken at the British serial killer Fred West's house during the height of his crimes (had digital photography been invented). This flexible scheme has the advantage over file signature approaches whereby it will identify other images outside the known images evidence base, i.e. unknown images. Therefore, it may be used to search for images that may record a crime that are available online but not known to the forensics examiner.

An issue that arises is the trade off between performance and RAM utilisation. That is to say, comparing a file with signatures that are preloaded into RAM will inevitably be faster than retrieving each signature from a database as it is needed. However, there will come a point for a given system when the number of signature objects loaded into RAM will become so big that it will be necessary to allocate some to virtual memory at the expense of performance. It is noted that reducing memory capacity is an important consideration for the development of commercially viable forensic tools (Collange et al, 2009). Thus, signatures are between 100 to 200 bytes and holding 100,000 signatures would require approximately 20 megabytes of spare RAM.

4. Case study and results

To demonstrate the applicability of the proposed approach, this section presents a case study of using MetaFor and discusses the results.

To assess the applicability of the approach, tests are carried out on two separate Web servers and utilise two groups of sixteen signatures. Firstly, the tests are applied to a 3.06 Ghz Intel Ei System development machine running an Apache Web Server. Running the tests locally eradicates any latency or network errors that may impose themselves on the results to give a more reliable assessment of the software itself with relatively constant response times. The second set of tests is carried out with the same images, but on a remote Website. These results are more realistic in terms of timings and network errors but response times could vary depending on network and Website traffic.

The Websites have the following features:

- A front page from which the search is initiated.
- Three picture galleries containing between six and ten identical images and text.
- Images that contain different file types (.png, .gif and .jpeg).
- Images that contain EXIF data and images that do not (including thumbnails).
- Two images that are identical.
- Top level menu with links to the three picture galleries.
- Secondary menu with the same links providing double circular links to all galleries.
- A broken link to an image that does not exist.
- A broken link to a web page that does not exist.
- Images that ranged from 30 kilobytes to nearly six megabytes.

The initial starting point of the search is then configured to point to each front page in turn and the crawl is initiated. The application is written with extra functionality that can be removed after testing. This functionality passes a job tracking object between each of the queues and timestamps the object as it finishes its work. Having a start and end time with each unit rather than just recording the end times prevents any confusion where threads are asleep waiting for another thread to relinquish control. This can report large processing times for a component that may have done its work very quickly. These objects are held in a chronological list and can be displayed via a reporting form. Furthermore, by taking the start time of the first object and the signature processing time of the last, we can deduce the overall time of the whole search.

The tests are run with a depth of two, meaning it will scour the front page and the pages that link from it, i.e. it will reach the gallery pages but will not follow links from thereon in. Table 1 presents the results of the signature matching against known signatures on both Web servers.

File Name	Signature present	Signature Matched
logo.png	N	-
feed.png	N	-
046.JPG	Y	10
2012-03-17%2013.48.55.jpg	Y	8
medium_2012-02-14%2008.28.08.jpg	N	-
2012-03-16%2014.12.53_0.jpg	Y	8
medium_2012-03-16%2014.12.53.jpg	N	-
IMG_0125.jpg	Y	6
medium_8.jpg	N	-
medium_2012-03-16%2011.10.03.jpg	Y	1
medium_135.JPG	N	-
IMG_0950.JPG	Y	23
medium_IMG_0953	Y	1
medium_IMG_0951	N	-
medium_IMG_0955	Y	1
edium_OtherSide.JPG	Y	1
whirlpool.jpg	N	-
medium_131.JPG	Y	1
medium_115.JPG	N	-
medium_094.JPG	N	-
medium_058.JPG	N	-
medium_046.JPG	N	-
medium_002.JPG	Y	1

Table 1: Results of signature matching

The results in table 1 suggest that images are matched against known signatures when they are present. Data to be matched to signatures is present in 11 of the files tested and these are detected by the scheme. In addition, no false positives were observed. It should be noted that this is a small data set. Future work will comprise much larger data sets of files and signatures. This is acceptable for a proof of concept, however, scaling the system for realistic use would mean thousands (if not hundreds of thousands) of signatures for comparison.

An advantage of the MetaFor approach is that the data required for the signature is located at the start of the file so the whole file does not have to be downloaded. Therefore, an image can be found, data downloaded and checked against a signature in an average of 149 milliseconds, or around seven per second on the local Web server. There is a slight increase for the remote Web server with an average of 261 milliseconds (less than four per second). Owing to the fact that the images may not be cached at the time of execution, these timings should probably be regarded as a best case scenario, and not typical.

There are a few interesting timings to note. First, the image processing time seems particularly low on the local Web server. Given that the size of the piece of the image file is 65000 bytes and the HTML/XML pages downloaded were between

1407 bytes and 8192 bytes it was expected that the processing time would be proportional. However the image downloads average around 10 milliseconds and the HTML around 300 milliseconds. Initially it was presumed that a program library was downloading asynchronously and that would explain the timings. However, further investigation into the code revealed that the start and end times must be being set before the download start and after it finishes. This behaviour is not seen on the remote server results and it is assumed that this is due to caching on the local Web server.

Second, the signature timings are unrepresentative of realistic execution times. When an image is found that has EXIF data the time reported for extracting the data and checking against the signatures is around 20 milliseconds. This test case only checks the extracted data against two groups of 16 signatures. A realistic number of signatures would be significantly higher, potentially in the order of several hundreds of thousands and this number could conceivably increase daily.

5. Conclusions and further work

Our continued reliance on the Internet as an information repository brings many benefits. However, it also gives rise to many concerns, such as the dissemination of illegal material, and in particular, indecent images of children, through social network sites and Web fora. This paper presents a novel approach, MetaFor, by which forensics examiners may run automated searches of remote Web servers for known illegal images by signatures formed from JPEG metadata. In this way, they are able to automatically detect repositories of illegal images or further sources of evidence. This approach differs from other signature schemes in that it uses file header metadata rather than image data to create the signature. In this way, MetaFor can be extended to search for unknown files. These files may support non-digital investigations, for example, searching for geographical and temporal signatures formed from the file metadata may identify digital pictures related to a traditional crime. Initial results presented in this paper, albeit on a small data set, demonstrate the applicability of the approach.

Future work aims to extend the tests to many more signatures to evaluate system performance. In this way, the potential issues of false positives and signature processing can be fully evaluated. Furthermore, as indicated in the results, performance issues in terms of Web server processing, in particular the discrepancy between image downloads and HTML processing, may also be assessed.

6. References

Access Data (2013). http://www.accessdata.com. (Accessed 10 January 2013).

BBC (2012), http://www.bbc.co.uk/news/uk-18181848. (Accessed 10 January, 2013).

Chang-Tsun Li & Yue Li (2012), "Color-Decoupled Photo Response Non-Uniformity for Digital Image Forensics", *IEEE Transactions on Circuits and Systems for Video Technology*, Volume 22 Number 2, pp. 260-271.

Collange, S., Dandass, Y. S., Daumas, M. & Defour, D. (2009), "Using graphics processors for parallelizing hash-based data carving", *Proceedings of the 42nd Hawaii International Conference on System Sciences (HICSS'09)*, Hawaii, USA, 2009, pp. 1-10.

Fan, J., Kot, A. C., Cao, H. & Sattar, F. (2011), "Modeling the EXIF-Image correlation for image manipulation detection", *Proceedings of the 18th IEEE International Conference on Image Processing (ICIP)*, Brussels, Belgium, 2011, pp. 1945-1948.

Guidance Software (2013). http://www.guidancesoftware.com. (Accessed 10 January 2013).

Haggerty, J. & Taylor, M. (2007). "FORSIGS: forensic signature analysis of the hard drive for multimedia file fingerprints", in IFIP International Federation for Information Processing, Volume 232, *New Approaches for Security, Privacy and Trust in Complex Environments*, Venter, H., Eloff, M., Labuschagne, L., Eloff, J. & von Solms, R. (eds.), (Boston, Springer), pp. 1-12.

Haggerty, J., Llewellyn-Jones, D. & Taylor, M. (2008), "FORWEB: File Fingerprinting for Automated Network Forensics Investigations", *Proceedings of e-Forensics 2008*, Adelaide, Australia, 2008.

Holleboom, T. & Garcia, J. (2010), "Fragment retention characteristics in slack space - Analysis and measurements", *Proceedings of the 2nd International Workshop on Security and Communication Networks (IWSCN)*, Karlstad, Sweden, 2010, pp. 1-6.

International Telecommunication Union (ITU) (1992), "Information Technology - Digital Compression and Coding of Continuous-Tone Still Images - Requirements and Guidelines. http://www.w3.org/Graphics/JPEG/itu-t81.pdf. (Accessed 10 January, 2013).

JEIDA (1998), "Design Rule for Camera File System, version 1.0, JEIDA-49-2-1998", http://www.exif.org/dcf.PDF. (Accessed 10 January 2013).

Kang, X., Li, Y., Qu, Z. & Huang, J. (2012), "Enhancing Source Camera Identification Performance With a Camera Reference Phase Sensor Pattern Noise", *IEEE Transactions on Information Forensics and Security*, Volume 7 Number 2, pp. 393 - 402.

Kee, E., Johnson, M. K. & Farid, H. (2011), "Digital image authentication from JPEG headers", *IEEE Transactions on Information Forensics and Security,* Volume 6 Number 3, pp. 1066-1075.

Mohamad, K. M. & Deris, M. M. (2009), "Single-byte-marker for detecting JPEG JFIF header using FORIMAGE-JPEG", Proceedings of the *Fifth International Joint Conference on INC, IMS and IDC (NCM'09)*, Seoul, South Korea, 2009, pp. 1693-1698.

Sportiello, L. & Zanero, S. (2011), "File Block Classification by Support Vector Machine", *Proceedings of the Sixth International Conference on* In *Availability, Reliability and Security (ARES)*, Vienna, Austria, 2011, pp. 307-312.

Visualisation of Allocated and Unallocated Data Blocks in Digital Forensics

C. Hargreaves

Centre for Forensic Computing, Cranfield University, Shrivenham, SN6 8LA, UK
e-mail: c.j.hargreaves@cranfield.ac.uk

Abstract

The ability to visualise blocks within file systems as allocated or unallocated is part of many existing forensic tools, for example the 'Disk' view in EnCase. However, analysis of the file system or partitioning of a disk is only one level of analysis that can occur as part of a digital investigation. Analysis of the structure within individual files can also be useful, however, there are limited examples of visualising file based data structures.

This paper provides a discussion of the development of a prototype visualisation tool that could be used for examining application or operating system files that themselves contain allocated and unallocated blocks. An example is provided that visualises the Windows Registry and demonstrates how a visualisation could assist in identifying areas that are unallocated and therefore may contain deleted data of interest. This approach has potential applications in teaching the binary structure of files and also for data recovery in situations where code exists to process the live data from a file format, but data carving strategies for that format have not yet been developed.

Keywords

Digital Forensics, Visualisation, Windows Registry

1. Introduction

Deleted data can be of importance in digital forensic investigations and some tools offer visualisations that can be used to highlight unallocated areas within file systems, and therefore may contain deleted data. This paper considers the visualisation of unallocated areas within files themselves.

The paper makes the following contributions: it demonstrates that a block based visualisation of the Windows Registry can show allocated and unallocated areas; and that tagging blocks and highlighting possible headers of deleted keys, in conjunction with visualising unallocated space, can show areas within files where deleted data is likely to be recoverable.

The paper is structured as follows: Section 2 provides background and related work, including consideration of an example visualisation, i.e. the EnCase 'Disk' view. Section 3 discusses the methodology for the paper and Section 4 provides the results. The results and method used are evaluated in Section 5, and Section 6 discusses conclusions and future work.

2. Background and Related Work

This section contains an overview of background material on allocated and unallocated blocks in file systems, the visualisation of block allocation in existing forensic tools and the importance of deleted data in digital forensic investigations.

2.1 EnCase 'Disk' Visualisation

One example of a block based disk visualisation can be found in EnCase, which can display blocks of a disk image based on the contents of a sector. An example is shown in Figure 1, which was generated using EnCase 6.19.7.2. The legend for the visualisation reveals that blocks can be tagged as 'Volume Boot', 'FAT 1', 'FAT 2', 'Root Folder, 'Unallocated', 'Bad Cluster', 'Allocated', 'Lost Cluster', 'Deleted File', 'Boot Sector', 'Wasted Area', 'No Partition', 'Unknown', 'Volume Slack', 'Disk Manager'.

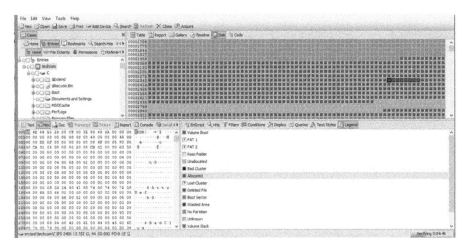

Figure 1: The 'Disk' view of EnCase

However, in digital forensics, different layers of abstraction are often referred to when discussing analysis. Carrier (2005) discusses several layers: Physical Storage Media Analysis, Volume Analysis, File System Analysis, Application/Operating System Analysis. EnCase can also be used to create a 'Disk' visualisation of some files that allow the 'View File Structure' option, for example the Windows Registry and PST files. This suggests that visualisation of data at other layers of abstraction, for example the Application/Operating System level is potentially of interest. However, there are several main limitations of this example representation. First is that there are a limited range of files that can be processed such that their internal structure can be displayed in this 'Disk' view. Secondly, the block size is predetermined; in this example, the block size is that of a sector (512 bytes). As will be investigated later, different values for block sizes may offer potential benefits. Finally, there are limited criteria for highlighting particular blocks, i.e. blocks are coded mostly on an allocated/unallocated basis.

2.2 Deleted Data

Deleted data is clearly of interest in digital forensic investigations, and the existence of the visualisation in EnCase suggests that displaying a visualisation of 'unallocated' blocks or clusters within a file system is of interest. The ability to view the blocks of files displayable using the 'View File Structure' option also suggests that visualising the internal blocks of files stored within file systems may be of use. There are several file types that have internal structures that may result in 'unallocated' blocks within the files themselves, for example the Windows Registry (Thomassen 2008), SQLite databases (Pereira 2009) or index.dat files (Jones 2003). Bespoke data recovery techniques exist or can be developed for extracting deleted data from many of these file formats (which can be referred to as data carving). There are parallels here with file carving, which can be applied to both partitions or compound files, and usually results in extracted files as output, but data recovery techniques applied to single files can also output text results or table-based data that represent recovered records. File or data carving is a substantial topic within digital forensics and space does not permit an extensive review in this paper. This paper focuses on creating a block-based visualisation of files that is capable of highlighting unallocated areas where deleted data may reside and applying additional criteria to suggest particular sections of unallocated that may warrant further examination.

2.3 Existing Visualisations

There are several existing visualisations available for binary files. Screenshots of these existing visualisations cannot be included due to space restrictions. However, a non-exhaustive summary is provided below.

Byte Frequencies: Tools such as WinHex (X-Ways Software) and 010 (Sweetscape Software) are capable of a graphical representation of the byte frequencies within a file. This can give an overview of the distribution of bytes, for example large portions of zero bytes, or an even distribution of all bytes.

Visualisation of Entropy: Another visualisation is based on the entropy of sections of data within a file. Cortesi (2012) allows areas to be highlighted that represent high entropy, for example encrypted data.

Comparison of Binary Files: There are also tools that will compare two files and offer a simple visualisation in the form of highlighting differences between the files, usually as a side-by-side comparison.

A further and thorough discussion of different binary file visualisation is available in Conti *et al* (2010). Conti also provides a table that discusses uses for binary file visualisation. Based on the discussion of these different uses provided in Conti, this paper focuses on visualisation for the tasks of "Locating and extracting metadata" and "Locating and extracting hidden content".

3. Methodology

3.1 Aim

The aim of this research is to investigate the visualisation of block allocation within application or operating system level files. Specifically the research seeks to determine if visualising blocks of such files potentially offers benefits to a digital forensic investigation.

3.2 Research Method

This research assumes that we are working with known/reverse engineered data structures that can be parsed. Therefore, some of the binary file visualisation techniques that could be applied would not provide any additional insight, for example byte frequencies. The approach taken in this paper is to focus on block-based analysis of files and graphically representing the allocated or unallocated nature of a block.

This exploratory research paper consists of a case study that focuses on a single file format, and involves the development of a software prototype that identifies the allocated/unallocated nature of a block and produces a graphical representation of these states. The development then focuses on adding more detailed block tagging and investigates the effect this has on the visualisations. There are two phases to the research presented in this paper; the first is data generation, and the second is data visualisation.

3.3 Data Generation

As stated in Marty (2008), "Visualization cannot happen without data or information. Therefore, before we can start talking about graphs and visualization, we have to talk about data". In the context of this paper, this means that in order to visualise the allocated or unallocated nature of blocks within a file, it is necessary to determine what certain areas of a file are being used for and to store this information.

There are many possible choices for a demonstration of block visualisation of an operating system or application file, for example: Windows Registry hives, Internet Explorer index.dat files, or SQLite databases could all be represented as blocks. In this case the Windows Registry has been chosen since the structure is complex but fairly well understood.

While the example given in Section 2 showed that EnCase is already capable of visualising allocated and unallocated blocks within the Registry, it does not allow more complex highlighting based on additional criteria. Also the block size chosen does not appropriately represent the granularity of the block size in the Registry, which could be divided up based on hbins (multiples of 4096 bytes), or cells (8 bytes).

Detailed descriptions of the Windows Registry binary format exist in Russinovich and Solomon (2009), Thomassen (2008), Norris (2009) and others, and due to space constraints the explanation are not repeated here. However, as an overview of the structures, the hive files (e.g. NTUSER.DAT, SYSTEM, SOFTWARE) are divided up into hbins, which are multiples of 4096 bytes. The hbins contain cells, which are multiples of 8 bytes, and these cells contain records of various types, e.g. *nk* (key records), *vk* (value records), various types of subkeys lists, value lists and actual data values.

Several parsers exist that are capable of processing the binary structure of the Windows Registry, for example Carvey (2013) (Perl based) and Ballenthin (2013) (Python 2 based). In addition the author of this paper also has previously created Python 3 based code for Registry hive processing, and since this code was the most familiar this was selected for use.

3.4 Data Visualisation

After enhancement of a Windows Registry parser in order to generate information regarding block allocation, the next phase is the visualisation of the data. The focus of the research in this paper is to provide a simple representation of block allocation within the data structure.

Despite focusing on applying a simple block-based visualisation, it is necessary to give consideration to factors such as block size and the technology used to implement the visualisation. There are a large number of possibilities for implementing a visualisation of the block allocation data. Much visualisation software is written in Java, but since the Registry hive processing was performed in Python 3, this was also used for the visualisation. There are several options for GUI based applications in Python, for example TkInter, GTK, PyQT. However, an approach was taken to make use of some of the features used by modern Web based applications. Instead of using Python GUI frameworks, Python can be used to start a web server on the local machine and the interaction performed though a web browser. This allows HTML, Javascript and CSS to be used to create the visualisation, with Python handling the data interpretation. While the visualisation used in this research is quite simplistic, the approach provides great flexibility for future alternative visual representations.

4. Results

This section provides more detail of the development process for the data generation and visualisation stages. It also provides sample results and discusses the adjustment of parameters to highlight particular areas of interest within the Windows Registry.

4.1 Data Generation

Section 3 discussed the selection of the Windows Registry for this visualisation and that a Python 3 based parser is used. The existing parser processes the *baseblock*, *nk*, *vk*, *li*, *lf*, *lh*, *ri* records of the Registry, in addition to the data nodes. *Sk* records were also added to the parser's processing list to increase the accuracy and coverage of allocated block identification. In terms of the block size for the Registry, since records are stored within multiples of 8 byte cells, an 8 byte block size was chosen. In order to record the status of blocks a simple data structure was created that allows blocks to be tagged with a particular a string to indicate its content.

While space restrictions in this paper considers tagging blocks within the Windows Registry only, the particular implementation was developed such that the principles could be applied to other block-based application or operating system files. In order to create an approach that could be generalised, the mechanism by which the raw data of the Registry hives was read was replaced with a new class that was capable of maintaining a record indicating the nature of the data contained within the block. The existing means of parsing the Windows Registry was to read the entire file into a list of bytes and to access sections of it using slicing. Reading whole files into memory in this case is an acceptable approach since even large Registry files are small enough that this does not pose a problem. To allow a record to be maintained of block use, a new class was created called `block_reader`. This requires a value to be passed to the constructor describing the block size to be used. In addition the class implements a `__getitem__(self, index)` method that means that the new class also allows slicing. Since this new class now operates in the same way as the old bytes object, the existing parser continues to work as before. Additional methods were added to allow blocks to be tagged with particular values.

```
tag_block_based_on_offset(offset_min, offset_max, tag)
```

Therefore an example new implementation for reading and processing the Windows Registry is (code has been restructured slightly for ease of reporting in this paper):

```
reg_key_data = reg_data[start_offset:start_offset + key_length]
type = self.identify_type(reg_key_data)
values = get_values(reg_key_data, type)
reg_data.tag_block_based_on_offset(start_offset,
                        start_offset + key_length, type)
```

The code in bold is the only change necessary to the existing parser code. This approach allows an internal list of blocks to be maintained and tagged with strings. Strings were chosen rather than simple Boolean values so that more sophisticated tags can be used for blocks rather than simply 'allocated' or 'unallocated'. While initially blocks were tagged as allocated or unallocated, additional tagging and the implications are discussed in Section 4.2.

4.2 Visualisation

After parsing of the Windows Registry files and creation of a map of blocks, the allocation of blocks needed to be visualised. As discussed in the previous section, Python was used to run a local web server, using HTML, Javascript and CSS to generate the visual interface. The approach that was used in terms of the HTML interface was to use SVG rather than Canvas. In terms of performance, the Canvas is more suited to the problem, however, since some interactivity is required, for example to perform an action on clicking a block, SVG is more appropriate since individually drawn elements can have their own event handlers. Interactivity with Canvas is possible through third party libraries, but this has not yet been explored. The developed map of block allocation requires that the colour is specified for blocks that are tagged with specific strings. In this code snippet, blocks tagged as unallocated are black (#000000), and all other blocks tagged with anything else are tagged green (#00FF00).

```
self.reg_block_map.add_block_colour("unallocated", "#000000")
self.reg_block_map.set_default_used_block_colour("#00FF00")
```

However, as was discussed in Section 3, it should be possible to produce more detailed visualisations on the block structure within files. To this end, the visualisation code was modified to tag the hbin headers as blue (#0000FF), which is also shown in Figure 2.

```
self.reg_block_map.add_block_colour("unused", "#000000")
self.reg_block_map.add_block_colour("hbin", "#0000FF")
self.reg_block_map.set_default_used_block_colour("#00FF00")
```

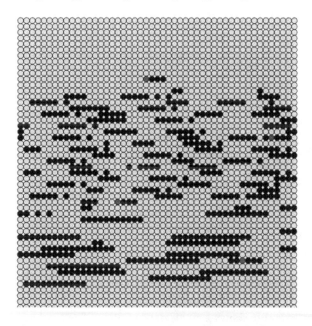

Figure 2: In this example the green cells are allocated and the black cells are unallocated. In addition the blue highlights indicate hbin headers

This clearly shows the hbin headers occurring every 4096 bytes (strictly speaking multiples of 4096 bytes). However, it is difficult to imagine a practical use for this outside of teaching the Registry binary structure.

The Python web server code, HTML and Javascript were modified to allow individual cells to be clicked and the contents of that cell displayed in a separate HTML div, through an AJAX request. The code was then enhanced in two further ways. Firstly it was modified so that when clicking a cell that is tagged as unallocated, rather than just displaying the contents of that cell, consecutive unallocated cells before and after the selected cell are also displayed. This allows more effective exploration of areas of unallocated space within the Registry hive. Secondly, the Registry parser was updated to perform a second pass of the hive after reconstructing the Registry hierarchy. During this second pass, the parser examines only the blocks marked as unallocated and scans for specified criteria. In this example a scan was conducted for *nk* records, simply by searching for an *nk* signature at offset 4 (decimal) into the cell. These cells were tagged as nk-del, and the visualisation was updated to highlight these cells in red. This is shown in Figure 3.

```
self.reg_block_map.add_block_colour("unused", "#000000")
self.reg_block_map.add_block_colour("hbin", "#0000FF")
self.reg_block_map.add_block_colour("nk-del", "#FF0000")
self.reg_block_map.set_default_used_block_colour("#00FF00")
```

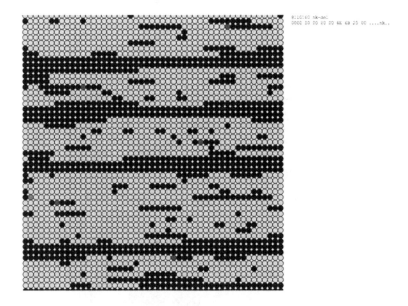

Figure 3: This example shows a single deleted nk header has been identified and highlighted in red. The hexadecimal view of the contents is displayed on the right after clicking the cell

However, it can also be seen just from the visualisation (i.e. without viewing the hexadecimal) that the cells immediately after the identified deleted *nk* record are allocated, and therefore the potentially useful information from the *nk* record e.g. the key name, has been overwritten by the cell that follows. However, in the next example it can be seen that the cells that follow the identified deleted *nk* record have been marked as unallocated and so there is potential for recovery. This is shown in Figure 4.

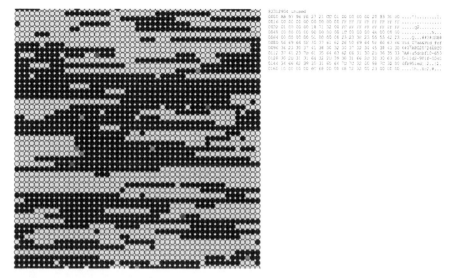

Figure 4: Deleted nk record headers are shown in red. The cells after one of them have been selected and the hexadecimal content is displayed on the right

As can be seen in the hexadecimal view of the recoverable nk record, the complete Registry key can be recovered, including key name and parent ID. Using this information, it can be determined that it is a deleted key from within the USB Enum key and contains a VID (07AB) and PID (FCF6) of an attached USB stick. Significant care must be taken in interpreting any deleted data and a thorough understanding of the binary structure of Registry keys should be sought before any conclusions drawn from the data displayed.

5. Evaluation and Limitations

This paper has demonstrated that visualisation of a block based operating system file using a block size that relates to its internal structure could offer potential benefit to digital investigations. It should be noted that this tool is a prototype that demonstrates a concept, rather than a software engineered final product.

In terms of evaluating the visualisation, no formal user study was conducted, so demonstration of the usefulness of the visualisation is supported only by the deleted *nk* record case study in the results section. A more thorough user study would be beneficial, including aspects of design including icons, use of colour, importance of speed of rendering, etc. This is particularly important in terms of drawing any conclusions about the effectiveness of the visualisation approach compared to automated criteria-based record carving such as those discussed in Thomassen (2008) or Morgan (2008). However, it may be possible that if a file format existed that could be parsed, but no data carving approach had yet been developed, this approach would allow those blocks that were not processed during the 'live' data parsing to be identified and inspected for data relevant to the case, or possibly used to assist in the development of a deleted data carving approach.

While this paper has shown that block based tagging and visualisation allows identification of areas of the Windows Registry that may contain recoverable information, this has not yet been extended to other block based file systems. To overcome this limitation, potential files that could be investigated include Internet Explorer index.dat files, SQLite databases and many others.

6. Conclusions and Future Work

This paper has shown that a block-based visualisation of the internal structure of the Windows Registry potentially offers insight into areas that may contain recoverable deleted data. The work certainly supports the sentiment in Conti *et al* (2010), which states "It is possible to create a visualization enhanced analysis system that combines the functionality of the best hex editors with the strengths of visualization." Combining the block-based visualisation with more interactive elements e.g. a keyword search followed by viewing the hit in context may also be of interest. This should also be expanded to other file formats, as discussed earlier. In addition a formal evaluation of the use of such visualisations should be conducted both for analysis and also for the teaching of binary structures of files. In any case, in order to facilitate any such visualisation, the internal structure of a file needs to be interpreted and the contents of blocks in some way recorded. This paper has demonstrated one mechanism by which this is possible.

7. References

Ballenthin, W. (2013) Python-Registry [online], *williballenthin.com*, available: http://www.williballenthin.com/registry/ [accessed 15 Feb 2013].

Carrier, B. (2005) *File System Forensic Analysis*, 1st ed, Addison-Wesley Professional.

Carvey, H. (2013) RegRipper [online], *regripper.wordpress.com*, available: http://regripper.wordpress.com/ [accessed 15 Feb 2013].

Conti, G., Dean, E., Sinda, M., Sangster, B. (2010) 'Visual reverse engineering of binary and data files', *VizSec*, 1–17.

Cortesi, A. (2012) Visualizing Entropy in Binary Files [online], *corte.si*, available: http://corte.si/posts/visualisation/entropy/index.html [accessed 15 Feb 2013].

Jones, K.J. (2003) 'Forensic Analysis of Internet Explorer Activity Files', *Web*, 1–30.

Marty, R. (2008) *Applied Security Visualization*, Addison-Wesley.

Morgan, T.D. (2008) 'Recovering deleted data from the Windows registry', *Digital Investigation*, 5(Supplement 1), S33–S41.

Norris, P. (2009) *The Internal Structure of the Windows Registry*. Cranfield University MSc Dissertation.

Pereira, M.T. (2009) 'Forensic analysis of the Firefox 3 Internet history and recovery of deleted SQLite records', *Digital Investigation*, 5(3-4), 93–103.

Russinovich, M.E., Solomon, D.A. (2009) *Windows Internals, 5th Edition*, Microsoft Press.

Thomassen, J. (2008) *Forensic Analysis of Unallocated Space in Windows Registry Hive Files.* University of Liverpool, MSc Dissertation.

Author Index

www.ingramcontent.com/pod-product-compliance
Lightning Source LLC
Chambersburg PA
CBHW051054050326
40690CB00006B/719